Mosaic
God with us

Copyright © 2012 Scripture Union
First published 2012, reprinted 2014

ISBN 978 184427 726 1

Scripture Union
207–209 Queensway,
Bletchley,
Milton Keynes, MK2 2EB
Email: info@scriptureunion.org.uk
Website: www.scriptureunion.org.uk

British Library
Cataloguing-in-Publication Data
A catalogue record for this book is
available from the British Library.

Original content from www.lightlive.org
Compiled and edited by
Christine Wright
Design by kwgraphicdesign
Printed by Malita Press

✎ Scripture Union is an international
Christian charity working with churches
in more than 130 countries.

Thank you for purchasing this book.
Any profits from this book support SU
in England and Wales to bring the good
news of Jesus Christ to children, young
people and families and to enable them
to meet God through the Bible and
prayer.

Find out more about our work and how
you can get involved at:
www.scriptureunion.org.uk (England
and Wales)
www.suscotland.org.uk (Scotland)
www.suni.org (Northern Ireland)
www.scriptureunion.org (USA)
www.su.org.au (Australia)

Contents

What is *Mosaic*?   5

How to run a *Mosaic* session   6

Mosaic bookshelf   7

ILLUSTRATED LETTERS
Learn about following Jesus from Paul's letters to young churches
- ■ Introducing: 'Illustrated letters'   8
- ■ No place like home *Philippians 2:25–30*   9
- ■ Freed to serve *Philemon*   15
- ■ Letters to a friend *2 Timothy 1:3–10; 3:14–17*   21
- ■ Learn and remember verse poster   28

Case study: Glass half-empty?   29
Rona Orme, Children's Missioner for Peterborough Diocese, gives 16 reasons not to be discouraged but positive about your work

PETER AND JESUS
Respond to the challenge of Jesus' offer of friendship
- ■ Introducing 'Peter and Jesus'   31
- ■ New way of life *Mark 1:16–20*   32
- ■ New understanding *Mark 8:27–30*   37
- ■ New perspective *Mark 9:2–13*   42
- ■ Old fears *Mark 14:27–31,66–72*   47
- ■ New start *John 21:15–19*   53
- ■ Learn and remember verse poster   59

BONUS All-age service
Peter – this is your life!   60
Mark 1:16–20; John 21:15–19; Joel 2:12,13

Mosaic clinic   65
Tips from ministry practitioners to help you make the most of your small group with a wide age range

ELISHA THE PROPHET
Be confident in God's power and learn to trust him
- ■ Introducing 'Elisha the prophet'   66
- ■ Powerful provider *2 Kings 4:1–7*   67
- ■ Powerful life-giver *2 Kings 4:8–37*   73
- ■ Powerful healer *2 Kings 5*   80
- ■ Powerful warrior *2 Kings 6:8–23*   87
- ■ Learn and remember verse poster   94

What's next?   95

What is Mosaic?

Scripture Union has been providing resources for people working with children in church settings for over sixty years.

As times have changed, so have the resources, of course. Where once 'Sunday School' was the highlight of the week for many children, today many other exciting activities compete with the events that churches provide. Where once school life was largely dull and mainly sedentary, today teachers have a vast range of ways of engaging children in the learning process. It is hard now for churches to 'compete' with all the opportunities and activities that fill the 21st-century child's life.

Yet Scripture Union still wants children to have the best resources to help them learn about God, decide to follow Jesus and grow in faith. This applies to children in churches both large and small, as well as those who have no contact with churches. We publish a range of resources to equip children's workers whatever their situation. This includes the *Light* range which has resources for different age groups from 3 to 14.

You told us...
You only have a few children in your group and you have a wide age range. Maybe there is a 3-year-old, two 7-year-olds, a 10-year-old boy and a couple of girls who will soon be 14. Buying the whole range of *Light* products would be much too expensive and it would be time-consuming to go through each product looking for suitable activities for your session each week. You need a flexible printed product which enables you to choose suitable activities that will work across the age group.

Settings where *Mosaic* works best...
- Many churches begin Sunday worship with all ages together. In other churches, everyone arrives together, but separate into adult and children's groups and meet together again for a final time of worship. *Mosaic* can be used in either of these scenarios when the number of children attending is too small to make the provision of separate age-groups practical.

- *Mosaic* could also be used where the premises in which children meet are limited so that it is impossible to provide more than one group.

- *Mosaic* would also be useful where there are few adults able to work with the children. (Of course, there should, for reasons of safety and child protection, always be at least two adults with CRB clearance with the children.) In this case, most of the activities can be done together, with separate, targeted activities for younger and older children later in the session.

- *Mosaic* would also be ideal if you are starting a new children's group and want a simple programme to work with.

How to run a *Mosaic* session

WHAT YOU GET

Mosaic is a flexible resource designed to give you a structured programme.

There are also extra ideas which you can add to suit the time you have available and the group you are leading. Some of the extra resources can be downloaded from the *LightLive* website at www.lightlive.org.uk. But even if you cannot access the website, this book provides all you need for 12 exciting and meaningful sessions.

Introduction
Each series of two to five sessions begins with essential Bible background to the passages you will be using with the children. There is also an important paragraph giving insights into how the series can be tailored to the children in your group.

Core programme
Four activities are provided as the basic template for each session – a way of exploring the Bible, a worship response, and two options which help the group apply the Bible teaching to their own lives.

Extension ideas
Three extension ideas are suggested to provide more targeted activities for younger (perhaps under-8s) and more challenging things for older children to do (perhaps those aged 10 and over). Obviously, abilities differ and you will have to direct individual children to the activities best suited to them. Fresh ideas are also suggested each session for the 'Learn and remember verse' of the series.

BONUS All-age service
For an occasion when adults and children meet together for worship, *Mosaic* provides a bonus all-age service in keeping with the theme of one of the three series in this book. More all-age services and service starters can be found in *The All-Age Service Annual*, available from Scripture Union.

Case studies
Advice designed to inspire and encourage you in your work – from a writer experienced in working with small churches.

Top Tips
Helpful advice for working with your mixed-age group can be found in the *Mosaic* clinic.

LightLive
Create a group on *LightLive* online (www.lightlive.org) and you will have access to a huge choice of resources for your group. The database is searchable by topic and Bible passage so that you will never be short of an idea for your group-time or special event!

Helpful resources
Look on page 7 for targeted recommendations of other Scripture Union titles which will supplement your programmes, provide ideas to help your group grow in faith and help you increase your confidence.

Every week online
You can enhance your weekly sessions with downloads including:
- 'Bible story picture': a regular activity for 2–7s (These are also available as photocopiable pages at the end of each session.)
- 'Audio Bible story': a regular audio Bible story for 3–7s
- 'Learn and remember': a PowerPoint of a Bible verse to learn, for 5–11s
- 'Presentation': an activity with animation for 11–14s

MOSAIC BOOKSHELF

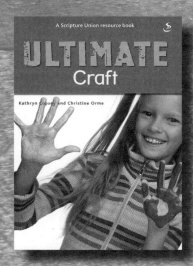

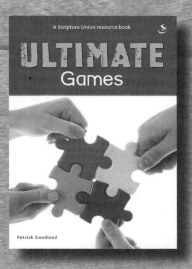

Ultimate Craft
£12.99
Ultimate Craft is crammed full of creative and imaginative ways to help you and your group explore the Bible through cutting, sticking, painting, drawing, sewing and, well, you get the idea!

Ultimate Creative Prayer
£9.99
Ultimate Creative Prayer is crammed full of creative and imaginative ways to help you and your children's group get praying.

Ultimate Games
£9.99
Ultimate Games is crammed full of creative and imaginative ways to help you and your children's group explore the Bible through playing games. Active games, quiet games, team games, individual games, games for children, games for young people – they're all here.

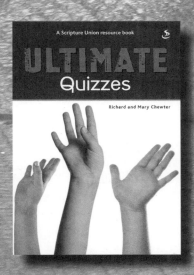

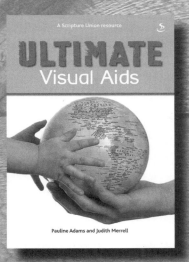

Ultimate Quizzes
£9.99
Ultimate Quizzes is crammed full of creative and imaginative ways to help your group explore the Bible through using quizzes.

Ultimate Visual Aids
£9.99
Open up the *Ultimate Visual Aids* CD-ROM and find a whole treasure trove of ideas to help you illustrate stories for children's groups, holiday clubs, all-age services and more. With drawings and pictures for use in activity sheets, OHP slides, presentations, banners, etc covering the whole Bible.

SERIES INTRODUCTION

ILLUSTRATED LETTERS

Learn about following Jesus from Paul's letters to young churches

BIBLE BACKGROUND FOR YOU
We look at three New Testament letters, written to deal with specific situations.

In Philippians Paul encourages the church to keep following Jesus. But serving Jesus can be costly, as Epaphroditus found. Yet even in his illness God still cared for him and looked after him. Paul expects the church to care for him as well – how well do we care for those who suffer?

Following Jesus requires change, which is why Paul encourages Philemon to take Onesimus back as a brother in Christ and forgive him: a massive challenge. How far are we ready to accept those who come from a different background or forgive those who have wronged us?

Paul encourages Timothy by reminding him of the truth of Jesus as we find it in the Bible, and the way in which it inspires, encourages, challenges and changes us. What are we doing to inspire the children in our groups to develop a passionate love for the Bible?

For your small group with a wide age range
We use Paul's letters to look at how God lives in his people, showing them goodness and mercy. Our older children will see that our relationships and outlook are very different from those who don't know God. Encourage younger children, who won't yet have this perspective, to feel they belong – this is so important to their understanding that they matter to God. Give scope for older children to realise that they can put what they are learning into action. In your group time, for instance, they can show care and acceptance for others who need their help and understanding.

Resources for ministry
The Bible is a key focus of this series. Get your 8–11s reading the Bible regularly with *Snapshots through the Year*. It encourages children to read

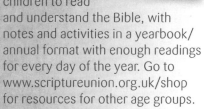

and understand the Bible, with notes and activities in a yearbook/annual format with enough readings for every day of the year. Go to www.scriptureunion.org.uk/shop for resources for other age groups.

Highlights from *LightLive*
Go to the 'Search *LightLive*' tab at www.lightlive.org and enter this session's Bible reference to find:

- 'Bible story picture': a regular activity for 2–7s
- 'Audio Bible story': a regular mp3 download for 3–7s
- 'Learn and remember': a PowerPoint of a Bible verse to learn, for 5–11s (see also page 28)
- 'Presentation': an activity with animation for 11–14s

SESSION 1

No place like home

Bible:
Philippians 2:25–30

Aim: To see that when God lives with his people they take care of each other.

CORE PROGRAMME

For 3–14s

Bible story in a letter

(20) *minutes*

Why: to see that when God lives with his people they take care of each other
With: a copy of the scroll (page 10), clue cards (page 11), a simple costume for a first-century Christian, SU *Bible Timeline* (all optional)

1 **Prepare**
In advance, copy the letter on page 11 and make it into a 'scroll', rolled up and if possible sealed with wax – it could also be made to look old by painting it pale brown or dipping it into cold tea.

2 **Talk about letters**
Find out from the group how they communicate with other people (for example, phone, email, text message). Challenge the children to find the entry for 'Paul's letters' on the *Bible Timeline*. Encourage them to imagine how Paul would

have sent his letters. Explain that, in biblical times, if someone wanted to send a letter they would write it on papyrus using a quill (feather) and then find someone they trusted to deliver it for them – they couldn't just put it in a post-box! Show the rolled-up scroll (if you have it) and ask how it differs from letters today (no envelope or stamp, but sealed with wax).

3 **Listen to the letter**
Dress in your costume, if you have one. Tell the children that you are one of the first Christians and that you live in Philippi. Explain that your church is very excited because you have received a letter from Paul, who was the first to tell you about Jesus. Open the letter and use the words to summarise Paul's letter to the Philippians and to tell the story of Epaphroditus. Remember to look at the children when explaining things, but to look down at the letter when reading. When you have finished, roll up the scroll and remove your costume.

4 **J O Y**
Write the letters 'J O Y' on a sheet of paper and ask the children what it says. Explain that, although Paul was in a horrible situation, his letter to the Philippians told them how happy he was and that they should be joyful, too. If you have Bibles, help the children look up and read

Philippians 1:4; 2:29; 3:1; 4:4,10. Say that 'joy' is certainly a theme for Paul!

Explain that Christians sometimes say that if you want to have real joy then you need to learn to put Jesus first, Others second and Yourself last.

Invite the children to say how they think Paul, the Philippians and Epaphroditus put Jesus first, others second and themselves last. For example, Paul and Epaphroditus put Jesus first by telling others about him; the Philippians put others before themselves by collecting money for Paul; Epaphroditus put himself last when he took the money to Paul and then worked so hard that he nearly died. You could use the cards numbered 1, 2, 4, 5, 6, 7, 8, 9, 10 and 11 from page 11 as clues for this.

5 **Challenge**
Challenge the children to say whether they would want to put Jesus first, others next and themselves last in their daily lives. Perhaps you could display the sheet of paper and invite the children to write their names on it if they want to follow Jesus and put him first, others second and themselves last. However, it might be best to let them do this after the session, so they make their own decision and do not simply follow their peers.

Bible story in a letter scroll

From Paul and Timothy, servants of Christ Jesus, to all God's people in Philippi.

Listen to this – Paul says that he prays for us with joy and thanks God for us because we have helped him in his work of telling others! Oh, but poor Paul, he's written to us from prison. The authorities don't like him telling others about Jesus and often have him arrested. This time they've taken him to Rome, and have put him under house arrest. That means that he can't leave the house and has people guarding him all the time – but at least he's allowed visitors.

Hey... he says here that, even though he's in prison, God is using it for good! How can being in prison be good? Oh, I see... most of the people visiting him are Christians and they spend their time talking about Jesus. He says that even the soldiers who are guarding him know about Jesus now – and not only that, the other Christians are leaving Paul and then telling people about Jesus with a lot more confidence. So the message is continuing to spread – hallelujah!

You know, because Paul was in prison we had a collection to get some money so he could buy food and things. Epaphroditus, one of the other Christians, took it to him and Paul says that everything arrived safely. I am pleased. It must have been a terrible journey for Epaphroditus – it's nearly 1,200 miles from Philippi to Rome, you know!

We've been so worried about Epaphroditus – he stayed on in Rome to help Paul, but then we heard that he was desperately ill. He had worked so hard telling others about Jesus and helping Paul that it took it out of him. Paul says that he nearly died! But now he's better, Paul has sent him back to us. One of the others saw him and said he's looking a lot thinner than he used to – but seems well nonetheless. He's the one who brought the letter from Paul to us.

Oh, it is so good to know that Paul and Timothy are all right. And Paul encourages us to keep running the Christian race because our reward will be with God in heaven. He says we should rejoice because good things are happening.

I haven't got time to read the rest of the letter now – I'll keep it for later. I'm so pleased to have it.

Clue cards

Cut out the cards. Number them on the back, and put each one face down in the correct order, with number 1 on the top.

1
Paul tells the Jews in Philippi about Jesus.

2
Paul is arrested in Jerusalem because he will not stop preaching.

3
Paul is sent to Rome where he is put under 'house arrest'.

4
The Philippians decide to have a collection to raise money to help Paul.

5
Epaphroditus is chosen to take the money to Paul in Rome.

6
Epaphroditus travels 1,200 miles to Rome.

7
After giving Paul the money, Epaphroditus stays on to help Paul.

8
Epaphroditus works so hard that he becomes ill and nearly dies.

9
Paul writes to the believers in Philippi to encourage them in their faith.

10
Epaphroditus recovers and Paul decides he should return home.

11
Paul writes to the church in Philippi and tells them to keep on going as Christians.

CORE PROGRAMME CONTINUED

Circle prayers

 5 minutes

Why: to thank God for each other

1 Recap the Bible story, emphasising who cared for whom and why. (Who did Paul care for? Who did Epaphroditus care for? Who did the church care for?)

2 Sit in a circle. Remind the children that you have been thinking about God's friends taking care of each other. Ask each person, in turn, to thank God for the person on their right.

3 Encourage the rest of the group to say 'Amen' after each prayer, as a sign that they agree with what has been prayed.

Ball of wool

 10 minutes

Why: to see that God lives with his people and that they take care of each other
With: a ball of wool or string

1 Invite the children to stand in a circle facing inwards. Briefly, review the ways in which the different people in the Bible story cared for each other.

2 Begin by holding the end of the wool and throwing the ball across the circle, so that it unravels as it goes. Say, 'God lives with (name of person you are throwing to).'

3 Encourage the person who catches the wool to hold on to the strand and throw the ball to someone else, saying, 'God lives with [name]'. You could do this two or three times.

4 Now you have a 'spider's web' of wool, say, 'God's people care for each other by…' (Invite volunteers to finish the sentence.)

Active game

5 - **10** minutes

Why: to think about how people travelled to different countries

1 Play a version of 'Port and Starboard', with the following actions:

- **Port** – run to the left side of the room
- **Starboard** – run to the right side of the room
- **Captain's coming** – salute
- **Sail for Philippi** – point to a corner of the room
- **Storm coming** – sway from side to side
- **Man overboard!** – hold nose and pretend to go under water
- **Land ahoy!** – shade eyes and look ahead
- **Row to shore** – make rowing actions

2 Say that today's Bible passage is about Paul's journey to take the good news to people in other countries who had not heard of Jesus.

EXTENSION IDEAS

Activities for younger children

Memory game

5 - **10** minutes

Why: to remember how people care for us

1 Ask everyone to sit in a circle, facing inwards.

2 Explain that you are going to play a memory game. Invite the first child to complete the sentence 'People care for me by…' (for example, playing with me or giving me presents). Encourage the second child to repeat that sentence and add their own ending, and so on.

3 The game gradually gets more difficult, so start with the younger children and finish with the leaders! You could have a second round, remembering people who care for us.

Bible story picture

Why: to experience God's loving care
With: a copy of page 14 (also available from *LightLive*) printed on A4 paper for each child, art and craft materials

1 Beforehand, prepare a named envelope for each child and put the Bible story picture inside. (Do not seal the envelopes.)

2 'Deliver' the envelopes to the children and let them take out the picture. Explain what the picture is about and how Paul wrote a letter about Epaphroditus.

3 When the children have finished their pictures, ask them to put them back in the envelopes for next time.

For older children

Sending postcards

5 - **10** minutes

Why: to encourage friends or church members
With: blank postcards, stamps (optional)

1 Give each child a blank postcard. Invite them to think of someone in the church they would like to give it to (encourage them to remember people they may not have much contact with, such as whoever cleans the church or arranges the flowers). Challenge them to decide what they could say to that person to help or encourage them.

2 Remind the children of the things that Paul said to the people in Philippi when he wrote to them – check out Philippians 1:2; Philippians 1:3,4; Philippians 1:8; Philippians 1:12,13.

3 Allow time for the children to write their cards. (They could copy out one of the Bible verses just mentioned.)

4 Encourage the children to give the postcards to the people concerned, or put stamps on them, address them and post them!

THE LEARN AND REMEMBER VERSE

'My grace is all you need, for my power is greatest when you are weak.'

2 Corinthians 12:9

Play a game of hangman by writing a dash for each letter of the verse. In turn, invite different children to suggest letters of the alphabet. Fill them in as they are selected, until the complete verse is revealed. Say it together.

Find a poster for this Learn and remember verse on page 28.

You could also use the song 'My Grace' on the *Bitesize Bible Songs 2* CD, available from Scripture Union.

Epaphroditus

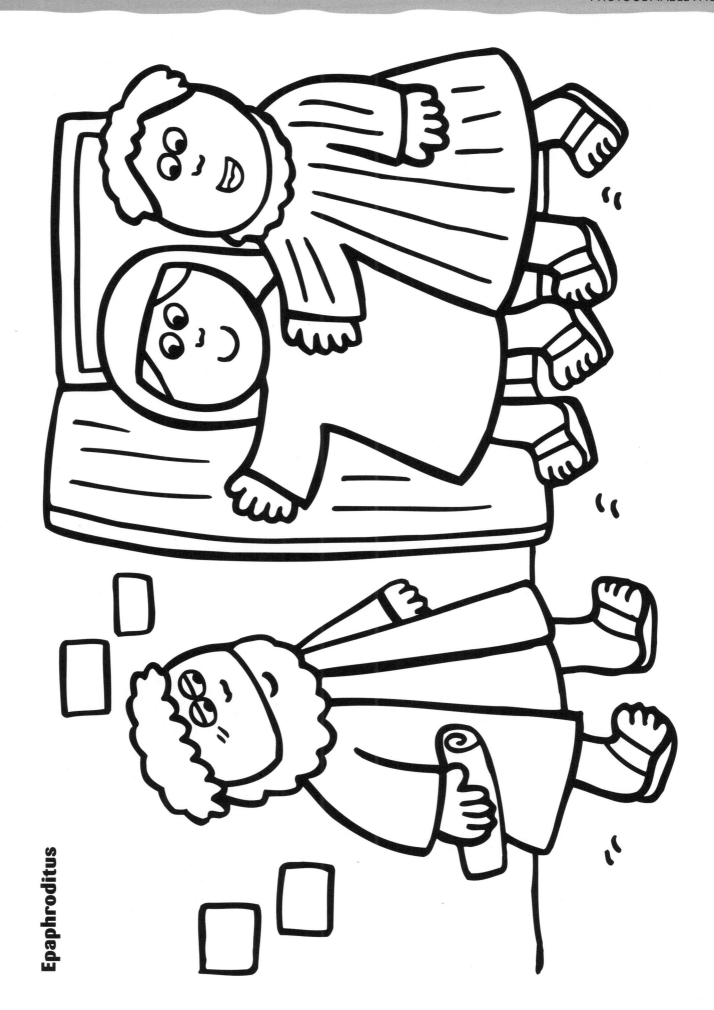

SESSION 2
Freed to serve

Bible:
Philemon

Aim: To discover that when God lives with his people, they forgive and accept each other.

CORE PROGRAMME

For 3–14s

Travelling Bible story

(15) – (20) *minutes*

Why: to discover that when God lives with his people, they forgive and accept each other

With: SU *Bible Timeline*, four large labels: 'Onesimus', 'Philemon', 'Paul's prison' and 'Philemon's house'

1 *Bible Timeline*

Cover up the words on the *Timeline* and ask the children to take turns to name some people in the pictures. When you have named as many as possible, uncover the writing and see how many more characters are mentioned.

Write out the names 'Onesimus' and 'Philemon'. Say to the children that some characters in today's story are not on the *Timeline*. Read their names together: Philemon (pronounced Fie-lee-mon) and Onesimus (Oh-nee-see-mus). Say that Paul is the other person in the story. Challenge the children to count how many times he is mentioned on the *Timeline*.

2 Set the scene

Explain that, at the time of the story, Paul was in prison, not for doing anything wrong, but because he kept telling people about Jesus. Display the label 'Paul's prison' at one end of the room.

Say that Philemon was a rich Christian, who lived a long way from Paul's prison. He and Paul were friends, although they may not have seen each other for some time. Display 'Philemon's house' at the other end of the room. Invite the children to join you there. (If you are short of space, place the labels at either end of a table and invite the children to walk between the two with their fingers, as appropriate.)

3 Act the story

Tell the children that you will be inviting them to act parts of the story as you tell it.

Story: Onesimus lived at Philemon's house, but he wasn't Philemon's friend: he was his slave. In those days it was common for people to have slaves. The slave belonged to the rich person and had to do whatever he was told. (Give some orders for the children to obey: 'Onesimus, sweep the floor... carry the food... pour the wine.')

Onesimus was not happy at Philemon's house and decided to run away. This was dangerous, because if he was caught he could be killed, so Onesimus was very cautious as well as frightened. (Invite a few children to creep, peering over their shoulders.)

Eventually, Onesimus arrived at the place where Paul had been staying. (Go to 'Paul's prison'.) Paul recognised him. Onesimus was scared (mime). But it didn't matter to Paul that Onesimus was a runaway slave. He made friends with him. Onesimus did lots to help Paul in prison. (Get the children to sweep and do other tasks.) Paul talked to him about Jesus (encourage the children to sit down, as if listening) and Onesimus came to love Jesus himself. When Onesimus knew that Jesus had forgiven him for the wrong things he had done, he felt he should go back and say sorry to Philemon, too. But would Philemon want to have Onesimus punished for running away?

Paul said he would write a letter to his friend, Philemon, to encourage him to forgive Onesimus. (Invite the children to pretend to write.) He gave the letter to Onesimus. They said goodbye, and Onesimus set off. (All walk back towards 'Philemon's house', and then stop suddenly. Ask the children to sit down.)

CORE PROGRAMME CONTINUED

4 **Time to think**

Say that this is all we know about the story. We can read Philemon's letter today (show it in your Bible). But did Philemon forgive Onesimus? Was Onesimus welcomed back?

Ask the children to think about the story. What do they think Philemon did? What would they have done? Now is their chance to talk to God about it.

5 **Pray together**

Ask the children to move to 'Philemon's house' if they think he forgave Onesimus, or back to 'Paul's prison' if they think he didn't. Finish with a prayer such as, 'Thank you, Jesus, that you forgive us. Help us to be ready to forgive others.'

Responsive prayer

 minutes

Why: to ask for God's help to forgive and accept each other

1 Teach the refrain: 'Help me to forgive and be friends.'

2 Ask the children to think about each line of the prayer below before joining in the refrain.

3 Say the prayer as follows:

When someone has hurt me,

Help me to forgive and be friends.

When someone has been unkind to me…

When someone has taken something of mine…

When someone has told lies about me…

When someone has stopped being friendly with me…

4 Give the children some time to reflect on this prayer, or to talk personally to God. Encourage them to remember this prayer during the week.

Make a banner

 **minutes**

Why: to remember that God lives with his people
With: a long sheet of paper with 'God lives with us' in bubble letters

1 Read the words on the banner together.

2 Encourage everyone to draw and cut out a picture of their face. Invite some children to colour in the letters on the poster. Challenge others to draw some pictures of some members of your church congregation.

3 Glue the faces on to the banner. Display the banner in a prominent position.

Think and chat

 minutes

Why: to realise that, although we're different, we can accept each other

1 Invite everyone to sit in a circle. Look at the child on your right and describe something about them that is different from you (for example, has long hair, has a sister or goes to school). Encourage that child then to turn to the next person and say something that they notice that is different about them. Continue round the circle.

2 Point out that, although we are all different, we can meet and have a good time together. God loves it when we accept each other and learn about him together.

EXTENSION IDEAS
Activities for younger children

Cut and stick

(8) *minutes*

Why: to think about how forgiveness may mean putting things right
With: pictures from pages 18 and 19, glue, scissors, sheets of paper

1 Give each child a copy of pages 18 and 19.

2 Remind the children that Onesimus had to put things right with Philemon. Onesimus said sorry. Sometimes, as well as saying sorry to God, we need to say sorry to other people and put things right.

3 Look at the pictures and identify the four 'wrong' pictures. Talk about what is happening. Cut them out and stick them on some paper. Talk about the other pictures and see how the wrong things are being put right. Cut out the pictures and stick them over the top of the matching 'wrong' pictures. Now the wrong things have been replaced by something good! Pray, 'Please help us to put things right.'

4 You could make up your own pairs of 'wrong' and 'right' pictures.

Bible story picture

Why: to be assured of the forgiveness of God
With: a copy of page 20 (also available from *LightLive*) printed on A4 paper for each child, art and craft materials

1 This is the second of three Bible stories taken from letters written by Paul. Beforehand, add the new Bible-story picture to the envelopes from last time. (Have spares available for children who come this time only.)

2 'Deliver' the envelopes to the children and let them take out the picture. Explain what the picture is about and how Paul wrote a letter to Philemon about Onesimus.

3 When the children have finished their pictures, ask them to put them back in the envelopes for next time.

For older children

Storytelling

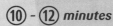 – ⑫ *minutes*

Why: to explore what 'forgiven' means

1 Tell this story of the boy and the broken vase:

A boy was helping his mum with the dusting. As he stretched to do the mantelpiece, he accidentally knocked over her favourite vase. It smashed into a million pieces. He realised at once that there was no way to fix it. He rushed out to the kitchen where his mum was making dinner. Sobbing, he confessed what had happened. Although she was upset that the vase was broken, his mum knew by her son's reaction that it was an accident. She went to help him clear it up. They wrapped the pieces in newspaper and put them in the dustbin. 'I know this was an accident. Don't worry, I forgive you,' she said, as she kissed her son.

She immediately forgot all about it, but the next day she found her son in tears. 'What's the matter? Are you hurt?' she asked.

'No, Mum,' he replied. 'Look, here are the pieces of the vase I broke. I'm so sorry.'

'Son, I have forgiven you for breaking the vase. Put the pieces back in the bin and forget about them.' However, the next day she found him crying over the pieces again.

2 Ask the whole group to discuss the following:

- What did the boy's mum mean by saying she had forgiven him?
- What did the boy understand by forgiveness?
- What do you think forgiveness means?

THE LEARN AND REMEMBER VERSE

'My grace is all you need, for my power is greatest when you are weak.'

2 Corinthians 12:9

Create a rhythm by slapping your thighs once, clapping once and then clicking the fingers on each hand. Then repeat the verse with one syllable on each click.

Find a poster for this Learn and remember verse on page 28.

You could also use the song 'My Grace' on the *Bitesize Bible Songs 2* CD, available from Scripture Union.

Cut and stick 1

Cut and stick 2

Philemon

SESSION 3

Letters to a friend

Bible:
2 Timothy 1:3–10;
3:14–17

Aim: To learn how important the Bible is from 'listening' to Paul writing to Timothy.

CORE PROGRAMME

For 3–14s

Bible story with paper scrolls

⑮ – ⑳ *minutes*

Why: to learn how important the Bible is from 'listening' to Paul writing to Timothy

With: three copies of the scroll (see page 22), SU *Bible Timeline* (both optional)

1 *Bible Timeline*

Roll up the scrolls from page 22 or quickly make three scrolls using rolled-up sheets of paper. Write the words 'Keep going' on the first sheet, 'Don't be ashamed' on the second and 'Read God's Word' on the third. Label the scrolls '1', '2' and '3'.

Invite the children to tell you anything they know about the Bible. If you have the *Bible Timeline*, look at the New Testament panels and see how many stories they recognise. Stop when you get to the picture of Paul. Explain that Paul had been travelling to many different countries telling people about Jesus, but now he was in prison. Ask the children how he could make sure that people still learned the truth about Jesus (he wrote letters to people he had visited). Show the children the rolled-up scrolls. Explain that, in the time of Jesus, people wrote their letters on sheets of papyrus and rolled them up. Say that you have a letter for a young man called Timothy and are going to deliver it to him.

2 Listen

Introduce another leader as 'Timothy', or read the part yourself:

'Hello, everyone. My name's Timothy. I grew up in a place called Lystra. My mother and grandmother told me about God and taught me to read the Scriptures – that is, God's Word. One day a believer called Paul came to Lystra. He invited me to go with him on his travels.

'But now Paul has been arrested and put into prison. I'm really worried. I'm so young; I don't know whether I'm clever enough to go on telling people about Jesus. Suppose I get put into prison too? Maybe Paul has some helpful advice.'

3 Read and listen

Ask one of the children to unroll the first scroll and read it out loud. Timothy should respond:

'Paul wants to remind me to keep going. He says that God has given me his Holy Spirit to help me to do the special job he's given me. So I mustn't be afraid – the Spirit will give me the power I need. That's good news, isn't it?'

Ask one of the children to unroll the second scroll and read it out loud. Timothy continues:

'Paul says I mustn't be ashamed to talk about Jesus. I do find it difficult sometimes. I worry that people might laugh at me or even try to hurt me. But Paul says I must use God's power. After all, the message is so wonderful. God is so kind that he sent his Son, Jesus, who died on the cross and rose again. No, I definitely won't be ashamed to tell people about Jesus.'

Ask one of the children to unroll the third scroll and read it out loud. Timothy then says:

'Paul wants me to keep on reading God's Word, the Scriptures. They are very useful for teaching us how to live our lives as God wants us to.'

4 Remember

Ask three children to stand at the front holding the scrolls. Invite them to read the words, then ask them to roll them up again. Ask the group whether anyone can remember the three messages.

Messages game scroll

CORE PROGRAMME CONTINUED

5 **Look in the Bible**

Explain to the children that, although Paul wrote to Timothy nearly two thousand years ago, we can still read the letters today. Show the children 2 Timothy in your Bible. Read 2 Timothy 1:8–10 and 3:14–17.

Ask the children what they have learned from Paul's letter to Timothy. Give them a few minutes to respond in prayer.

Messages game

 minutes

Why: to hear what God says in the Bible
With: copies of the scroll (see page 22), copies of the verses on page 24 (optional)

1 Give each child a copy of the scroll (page 22) and ask them to copy out a 'message from God' from page 24. (Make sure they use the scroll in landscape and roll it in from the sides.) Ask the children to roll up their sheets of paper from both ends, to make scrolls.

2 Invite everyone to sit together in a circle and begin to pass the scrolls round from hand to hand. Signal to stop passing the scrolls, call out the name of one child and help them to read the words on their scroll aloud.

3 Repeat, reading out and passing on the scrolls until all the messages from God have been heard.

4 At the end of the game, suggest everyone keeps the scroll they are now holding.

Letters

 **minutes**

Why: to experience an encouraging letter
With: envelopes

1 In advance, prepare an envelope addressed to each child containing an encouraging message, such as: 'I like the way you join in the worship.'

2 Place the letters in the middle of the group. Invite the children to take it in turns to pick up an envelope, read the name on it and give it to that person. When everyone has their letter, invite them to open and read it. Ask the children how their letter made them feel.

3 Say that today they are going to look at a letter in the Bible that was written to encourage a young man called Timothy.

Messages in worship

⑩ – ⑮ **minutes**

Why: to send worship messages to God
With: three envelopes; *Light for Everyone* CD and CD player or the written music from page 25 to play yourself; 'Thank you', 'Sorry' and 'Please' written on three separate sheets of paper

1 Place one of the words 'Thank you', 'Sorry' or 'Please' in each of the envelopes, and number the envelopes 1, 2 and 3 (so that 'Thank you' is in envelope 1, etc).

2 Ask the children how God speaks to us (through the Bible, prayer, other people, his Holy Spirit). Explain that, just as God speaks to us, he wants us to speak to him.

3 Sing 'Deep love' from the *Light for Everyone* CD. Repeat the song, pausing after the first verse to open the first envelope. Ask the children to imagine they are sending a message to God. What would they say 'Thank you' for? Allow them to pray aloud or silently.

4 Go on to the second verse and repeat the activity with the other

Deep love

God's deep love,
Always there.
God loves everybody everywhere.

God loved the people
On the earth so long ago,
God loves our families,
And everyone we know.

God shows his love to us,
So that's why Jesus came.
Because we've done things wrong,
He died to take the blame.

God's love is all around,
He's with us every day.
His Holy Spirit comes,
To help us live God's way.

© Nick Harding 2004, administered by Scripture Union

Messages game verses

"I know, LORD, that you are all-powerful; that you can do everything you want." Job 42:2

"O LORD, our Lord, your greatness is seen in all the world!" Psalm 8:1

"I have confidence in your strength; you are my refuge, O God." Psalm 59:9

"The Lord is good; his love is eternal and his faithfulness lasts for ever." Psalm 100:5

"He supplies the needs of those who honour him; he hears their cries and saves them." Psalm 145:19

"Trust in the LORD with all your heart. Never rely on what you think you know. Remember the LORD in everything you do, and he will show you the right way." Proverbs 3:5,6

"The Lord is like a strong tower where the righteous can go and be safe." Proverbs 18:10

"Holy, holy, holy! The LORD Almighty is holy! His glory fills the world." Isaiah 6:3

"Call to me and I will answer you; I will tell you wonderful and marvellous things that you know nothing about." Jeremiah 33:3

"Come back to the LORD your God. He is kind and full of mercy; he is patient and keeps his promise; he is always ready to forgive and not punish." Joel 2:13b

"He has provided for us a mighty Saviour." Luke 1:69a

"For God loved the world so much that he gave his only Son, so that everyone who believes in him may not die but have eternal life." John 3:16

"My grace is all you need, for my power is greatest when you are weak." 2 Corinthians 12:9

"All things are done according to God's plan and decision; and God chose us to be his own people." Ephesians 1:11

"Don't worry about anything, but in all your prayers ask God for what you need, always asking him with a thankful heart." Philippians 4:6

"God's Spirit fills us with power, love and self-control." 2 Timothy 1:7

"God has said, 'I will never leave you; I will never abandon you.'" Hebrews 13:5b

"Come near to God, and he will come near to you." James 4:8

"Listen! I stand at the door and knock; if anyone hears my voice and opens the door, I will come in and eat with them, and they will eat with me." Revelation 3:20

"'Now God's home is with human beings! He will live with them, and they shall be his people.'" Revelation 21:3

Deep Love

Nick Harding

2. God shows his love to us,
   So that's why Jesus came.
   Because we've done things wrong,
   He died to take the blame.

3. God's love is all around,
   He's with us every day.
   His Holy Spirit comes,
   To help us live God's way.

EXTENSION IDEAS

Activities for younger children

Chinese whispers

 minutes

Why: to learn how important it is to write messages down

1 Invite everyone to sit in a circle. Whisper the whole of 2 Timothy 1:9a to the child on your left and ask them to whisper it to the next child, and so on. Encourage the last child to say out loud what they believe the verse to be.

2 Say that just speaking messages means they might get changed. Ask the children what might be a good way of everyone knowing the verse correctly (writing it down, reading it from the Bible). Explain that the first Christians wrote down things about Jesus so that everyone could read them.

Bible story picture

Why: to discover that God's book, the Bible, includes letters to help us know more about living God's way
With: a copy of page 27 (also available from *LightLive*) printed on A4 paper for each child, art and craft materials

1 This is the third of three Bible stories taken from letters written by Paul. Beforehand, add the new Bible story picture to the envelopes from last time. (Have spares available for children who come this time only.)

2 'Deliver' the envelopes to the children and let them take out the picture. Explain what the picture is about and how Paul wrote letters to his young friend Timothy.

3 When the children have finished their pictures, ask them to put them back in the envelopes and to take them home so they can show their envelopes and pictures to family and friends.

For older children

Creative response

 **minutes**

Why: to get to grips with the Bible verses about the good news of Jesus

1 In twos or threes, with a leader if possible, ask the children to find and read 2 Timothy 1:9,10.

2 Say that this is the good news that Paul was in prison for. Challenge the children to work out a creative or dramatic way of presenting these verses. Perhaps they could say a line each, or work out a mime or some actions to accompany the words.

3 Allow time for them to work on this, and then invite each group to present the verses to the rest of the children.

THE LEARN AND REMEMBER VERSE

'My **grace** is all you need,
for my **power**
is **greatest**
when you are **weak**.'

2 Corinthians 12:9

Explain that 'grace' is when God is loving and kind to us, even though we don't deserve it. Say the verse in four sections (as marked) and encourage the children to think of actions for each of the words in bold.

Find a poster for this Learn and remember verse on page 28.

You could also use the song 'My Grace' on the *Bitesize Bible Songs 2* CD, available from Scripture Union.

Paul

'My grace is all you need, for my power is greatest when you are weak.'

2 Corinthians 12:9

CASE STUDY
Glass half-empty?

Rona Orme is not discouraged about working with just a few children. Instead she encourages us to celebrate the positive things about it.

Sometimes we can feel a bit discouraged that we only have a few children in our group. And sometimes other people can discourage us by pointing out that so few children come along. There can be a suggestion that you are 'not doing it right' or otherwise there would be more youngsters taking part. In the same way, it is easy to blame poor, cramped facilities or lack of resources for what is or is not happening. This is the glass half-empty approach. But how about looking at things the glass half-full (or even the 'glass full to the brim' that we are told about in Psalm 23) way? Learn to celebrate all the positive advantages of working with a few children, and give thanks to the Lord for blessing you in this way.

1 You can get to know the children, and their families, really well. You will be able to remember which child told you they were worried about going to the dentist – and have a follow-up conversation next time you see them. Relationships are the single most important factor in encouraging children to grow in faith. In a small group you start with a considerable advantage.

2 You can pray for each child by name during the week.

3 If one child's attendance drops, you have time to contact them and their family and encourage them back to the group. A visit to their home is a powerful message about the value of that child.

4 If the children who come to your group have a wide spread of ages, fewer children mean that you can focus what you do on the needs of those children. This is much more difficult when there are several age-ranges in a larger group.

5 You can have individual children in mind as you plan your session and activities. You will know if a particular child hates balloons or does not want to read aloud.

6 With fewer in the group, everyone can have a good turn at the activities – adults included.

7 You can take more risks with activities because you will waste less time on 'crowd control'. You can use paints in even the tiniest meeting space if there are only a few children to supervise.

8 You will need fewer resources so you may be able to buy better quality items – or just make do with a lower budget.

9 Everyone can see the illustrations in the book you are sharing.

10 There is time for everyone to answer a question or share their view. There is time to value the thoughts of all. The occasions when I have heard a child make a really telling contribution that challenged my own understanding of the things of God have all happened in a small group.

11 A small group with a range of ages can operate 'family-style', with older children learning to nurture and encourage younger ones, whilst younger children absorb the role-modelling of the older ones.

12 There will be more opportunities for children to take a lead.

13 Shyer children may blossom in a smaller group.

14 It is easy to watch a DVD on a laptop rather than having to worry about whether the projection system will work.

15 It is easier to organise an occasional treat or outing. A trip to a 'Praise Party' organised by a larger church, for example, will not require so many cars or accompanying adults.

16 Lastly, and most importantly, Jesus tells us that where two or three gather together, he promises to be with them (Matthew 18:20). You do not have to have a big group to have Jesus with you!

Rona Orme is Children's Missioner for Peterborough Diocese

SERIES INTRODUCTION

PETER AND JESUS

Respond to the challenge of Jesus' offer of friendship

BIBLE BACKGROUND FOR YOU

Peter has moments of great insight and great faith. He has times of abject failure. Through it all he is learning more about the love of God as he finds it in Jesus.

We start with his call. Jesus is doing something radical. Jewish rabbis waited for potential disciples to apply and then tested them. Jesus chooses his disciples. It must have been a little unnerving for Peter, especially leaving all that is familiar.

His recognition of who Jesus is forms a watershed in the Gospel story. It stems from all that he has seen and heard, but as Matthew's version makes clear, it has been revealed by God. The transfiguration confirms it. But despite this significant level of understanding, Peter does not always get it right – the low point is his denial. Peter was haunted by a sense of failure, so it is all the more wonderful that Jesus assures him that he is forgiven and restored to friendship with a job to do for him.

Most of us can identify with Peter in some way. So we need to ask: What can we learn from Peter about the way that we relate to Jesus? About the nature of Jesus? About how we show our love for him?

For your small group with a wide age range

As we follow Peter through this series, we see he was a close friend of Jesus. Even so, he didn't always get things right. Your group will therefore see just what it means to follow Jesus through good times and bad. Like Peter, the children can choose to follow Jesus and accept his ways – and the series offers opportunities for response.

Remember, however, that a younger child's simple, spontaneous response is unlike that of an older child who is capable of reasoning and a deeper commitment. Bear in mind that any positive response to Jesus is valued by him!

Resources for ministry

Top Tips on Helping a child respond to Jesus identifies four ways in which people like Peter responded to Jesus in the New Testament. It shows that we are all individuals and come to Jesus in the way that best suits us and our backgrounds.

Highlights from *LightLive*

Go to the 'Search *LightLive*' tab at www.lightlive.org and enter this session's Bible reference to find:

- 'Bible story picture': a regular activity for 2–7s
- 'Audio Bible story': a regular mp3 download for 3–7s
- 'Learn and remember': a PowerPoint of a Bible verse to learn, for 5–11s (see page 60)
- 'Presentation': an activity with animation for 11–14s

SESSION 1
New way of life

Bible:
Mark 1:16–20

Aim: To discover that Jesus wants people to follow him

CORE PROGRAMME

For 3–14s

Bible rap

⑮ – ⑳ *minutes*

Why: to discover that Jesus wants people to follow him
With: SU *Bible Timeline* (optional)

1 Bible

Help the children to find Mark's Gospel in their Bibles. Start at the beginning of chapter 1 and challenge them to summarise what has happened so far in the Gospel, using the subheadings in the Bible. If you have a *Bible Timeline*, when they get to Mark 1:16, stop and challenge them to decide where on the *Bible Timeline* this passage might fit. Then invite the children to follow in their Bibles as you read Mark 1:16–20, or ask for volunteers to read it.

2 Followers' rap

Set up a rhythm, with the children clapping their hands or tapping their knees. Read the following rap, one line at a time, and ask the children to repeat each line. Note that the rhythm changes for every third line.

**Out catching fish on the lake
  one day,
Casting their nets in the water
  of the bay,
It's Simon Peter and Andrew,
  you see.**

**Who do they meet on the beach
  that day?
Who do they meet on that bright
  fine day?
It's Jesus, who says,
  'Come, follow me.'**

**Leaving their nets in their boat
  to stay,
Peter and Andrew, they follow
  right away.
Following Jesus, who says,
  'Come, follow me.'**

**Sitting in their boats on the lake
  that day,
Cleaning their nets in their
  usual way,
It's James, and his brother
  John Zebedee.**

**Leaving their nets in their boat
  to stay,
James and John, they follow
  right away.
Following Jesus, who says,
  'Come, follow me.'**

3 Response

Ask the children how they think the fishermen might have felt that day. How might they feel if Jesus did the same thing to them today? Say that, although Jesus doesn't walk around on earth in the same way now, he still wants us to follow him, to be like him and to help other people follow him too. Invite the children to say how this makes them feel. It may be appropriate to spend a few moments in quiet to respond to Jesus' desire for us, his followers, today.

4 *Bible Timeline*

Ask the children to find the names of the men in today's story on the *Bible Timeline* (if you have one). Say that, for these men, this was just the beginning of their grand adventure with God, which the children are going to find out more about over the next few sessions.

Hunt and respond

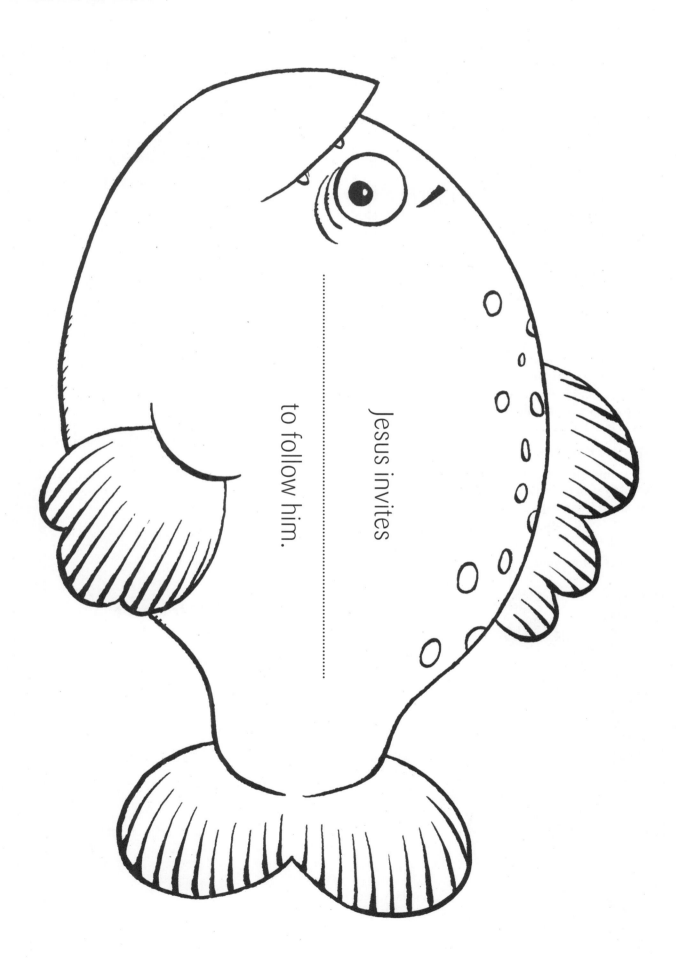

Jesus invites .... to follow him.

CORE PROGRAMME CONTINUED

Prayer

(5) *minutes*

Why: to thank Jesus that he wants us to follow him

1 Stand together, marching on the spot. Lead the prayer below. Ask the children to listen for when you say, 'Jesus is calling us', and to respond with, 'We will follow him!'

2 Pray:
Heavenly Father, Creator of the universe, we thank you that you sent your Son, Jesus, to earth. As Jesus walked by the lake, he called the fishermen to follow him. Jesus is calling us…

We will follow him!

Peter, Andrew, James and John left their fishing nets and followed Jesus. Please help us to leave behind anything that distracts us from following you. Jesus is calling us…

We will follow him!

Jesus told the fishermen that he would teach them how to catch people. Please help us to tell others about you, too. Jesus is calling us…

We will follow him!

Hunt and respond

(10) *minutes*

Why: to understand that Jesus wants people to follow him
With: Invitations for 'Hunt and respond' (see page 33), recording of 'The Servant King' (or another song about following Jesus) and means to play it

1 Before the session, hide an invitation for each child around the room.

2 Tell the children that something has been hidden in the room for them. Give them some time to find their invitations.

3 Ask how it feels to receive an invitation. Explain that, just as Jesus invited the fishermen to follow him, he invites us to follow him too.

4 Play the song, encouraging the children to sit quietly and tell God if they are ready to actually say 'Yes' to his invitation, or if they want to think about it.

5 Be available for any child who wants to talk further about following Jesus.

Obstacle course and prayer

(10) *minutes*

Why: to learn how to follow
With: blindfolds or scarves, bean bags or cushions

1 Before the session, design a simple, safe obstacle course using soft materials such as cushions and bean bags.

2 Encourage the children to work in pairs – one child is blindfolded while the other guides them around the course. It will probably be best to let the older ones guide the younger ones, or for the leaders to guide the children.

3 Explain that following Jesus isn't always easy. Say that someone guided us around the obstacles. Similarly Jesus helps us in difficult times. Pray, thanking Jesus for leading us every day. End with the children saying, 'Jesus, help us to follow you.'

EXTENSION IDEAS

Activities for younger children

Creative prayer with drawing

(5) - (10) *minutes*

Why: to respond to Jesus' call to follow him, or think about it some more

1 Talk about how Jesus found the fishermen busy doing their usual work. Ask the children to name some things they do every day.

2 Give each child a sheet of paper. Ask them to draw a line down the middle of their paper. On one half, invite them to draw a picture of themselves doing something that they do every day.

3 Ask the children what they would do to show other people that they follow Jesus. Then invite them to illustrate that on the other half of the paper.

4 End with a prayer that God will help us to be ready always to follow Jesus.

Bible story picture

Why: to find out about being a friend and follower of Jesus
With: a copy of page 36 (also available from *LightLive*) printed on A4 paper for each child, art and craft materials

1 Look at the picture together and decide which person is Jesus (on the left), and which is Peter. What do the children think is happening in this picture? (Jesus and Peter are meeting; Jesus is asking Peter to be his friend.) Look at the other items in the picture and work out that Peter's job was fishing: find a net, count the fish.

2 Colour in the picture of Jesus. What is he saying to Peter? Use the children's suggestions or all say: 'Hello, Peter. Come with me and be my friend.'

3 If the children think Peter will say 'yes', they can colour him in too. If they think he will say 'no' or if they are not sure, leave him plain. After reviewing the Bible story and seeing what Peter answers, allow time for children to go back to their pictures and colour in Peter, if they would like to.

For older children

Exploring calling and gifts

(15) *minutes*

Why: to help the young people think about what Jesus wants them to do
With: paper, felt-tip pens

1 Give each young person a sheet of paper and access to felt-tip pens. Ask them to write their name in the middle of the sheet of paper.

2 Explain that Jesus calls all of us to follow him, and this means following him in what we do. Encourage the young people to write or draw things that they enjoy doing, things that others ask them to do or perhaps things that they think God wants them to do. Your aim here is to draw out that Jesus called Simon to 'fish for people' because Jesus wanted Peter to use what he already knew about and was good at, to serve him. Challenge the young people to think about how they could serve God using their talents, skills and the things they like doing.

3 During this activity, make sure leaders are available to spend some time with each young person and explore how they might develop for God's glory any gifts or abilities they may have.

4 Close in prayer, asking God to help each person to follow him in the way that they can serve him best.

THE LEARN AND REMEMBER VERSE

'**Come back** to the LORD your **God.** He is **kind** and full of **mercy**; he is **patient** and keeps his **promise**; he is always ready to **forgive** and not **punish.**'

Joel 2:13b

Read the words of the verse from the poster on page 59. Challenge the children to invent actions for the keywords (shown in bold). Say and act out the verse together, challenging the children to remember it next time you see them.

You could also use the song 'Come back' from the *Bitesize Bible Songs* CD, available from Scripture Union.

Peter meets Jesus

SESSION 2
New understanding

Bible:
Mark 8:27–30

Aim: To explore how Jesus helps us know who he is.

CORE PROGRAMME

For 3–14s

Bible story with march

(20) minutes

Why: to explore how Jesus helps us know who he is
With: SU *Bible Timeline* (optional)

1 Walk
Tell the children that you are all going for a walk together. (If space is limited, the children may walk on the spot, or use their fingers to pretend to walk.) As you walk, ask the children questions about yourself, such as: What is my middle name? How old am I? What is my favourite food? Do I have a dog? Tell the children that people who spend time with you would know the answers to these questions.

2 Create
Walk up to the *Bible Timeline*. Point out the picture of Jesus teaching. Help the children to recreate this illustration as a living picture, using themselves as the characters. If you are not using the *Bible Timeline,* ask the children to pretend they are the disciples sitting down to listen to Jesus telling a story.

3 Listen
While the children are still, read the Bible story below:

Jesus and his disciples went to the villages near the town of Caesarea Philippi. As they were walking along, he asked them, 'What do people say about me?' The disciples answered, 'Some say you are John the Baptist, or maybe Elijah. Others say you are one of the prophets.' Then Jesus asked them, 'But who do you say I am?' 'You are the Messiah!' Peter replied. 'The one God sent to save his people!' Jesus warned the disciples not to tell anyone about him.

4 Marching rhyme
Say that you are now going to pretend to walk to the town of Caesarea Philippi, just like Jesus did in the story. Use the following rhyme to get a walking rhythm going. (Again, if space is limited, the children may walk on the spot, or use their fingers.) As you walk, do the actions in the rhyme:

**Step, step, slide, slide;
We don't have a car to ride,
Clap, snap, step again;
We can walk in sun or rain.**

Stop and ask the children who some people thought Jesus was (John the Baptist).

**Step, step, slide, slide;
We don't have a car to ride,
Clap, snap, step again;
We can walk in sun or rain.**

Stop and ask the children who other people thought Jesus was (Elijah).

**Step, step, slide, slide;
We don't have a car to ride,
Clap, snap, step again;
We can walk in sun or rain.**

Stop and ask who Peter thought Jesus was (the Messiah).

5 Reflect
Discuss how Peter knew who Jesus was. (It was because he had spent time with Jesus.) Other people didn't know because they hadn't spent enough time with Jesus. Ask the children to close their eyes and imagine they are one of the disciples walking with Jesus. Say a prayer thanking God for sending Jesus to spend time with his disciples so they could truly know him.

CORE PROGRAMME CONTINUED

Jesus prayer

 minutes

Why: to declare that Jesus is the Son of God

1 Say this active prayer together. Ask the children to shout, 'Jesus is the Son of God!' when you clap your hands. Practise shouting, 'Jesus is the Son of God!' on the signal, first. Then say:

Jesus did amazing, wonderful things because…
(Clap, clap!)
Jesus is the Son of God!
He helped people everywhere he went because…
(Clap, clap!)
Jesus is the Son of God!
People asked his friends, 'Who is Jesus?' They said…
(Clap, clap!)
Jesus is the Son of God!
Jesus asked Peter, 'Who am I?' Peter said…
(Clap, clap!)
Jesus is the Son of God!
Today we know who Jesus is…
(Clap, clap!)
Jesus is the Son of God!

2 A little while later ask the children, 'Who is Jesus?' and see what they answer. Repeat the last two lines of the prayer.

Collage

 minutes

Why: to look at how Jesus spent time with his friends
With: a large sheet of paper, a copy of the pictures for 'Collage' from page 39

1 In advance, write 'Jesus and his friends' on the sheet of paper and cut out the pictures.

2 Invite everyone to sit in a circle. Put the pictures face-up in the centre.

3 Ask the children to take it in turns to choose a picture and say what Jesus is doing. Encourage them

to stick their picture on the large sheet of paper. Give hints where necessary.

4 Tell the children that all the pictures show Jesus spending time with his friends so that they could find out who he really was.

True or false

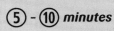 minutes

Why: to see what we know of Jesus

1 Before the session, write 'True' and 'False' in large letters, one each on a sheet of A4 paper.

2 Place the 'True' and 'False' signs at opposite sides of your room and invite the children to stand in the middle.

3 Read out some statements about Jesus and challenge the children to decide whether they are true or false. They should run to the appropriate side of the room when you say 'Go!' after each one. For example: Jesus was a fisherman (false); Jesus was a Jew (true); Jesus healed people (true); Jesus called Peter while he was shopping (false); Jesus was 30 when he started preaching (true). (Use this activity to recap on the previous session.)

Collage

EXTENSION IDEAS

Activities for younger children

Prayer

 minutes

Why: to ask God to help us know him better

1 Ask the children how Jesus' friends got to know him. (By spending time with him, listening to him and watching him.)

2 Chat with the children about the things the disciples saw Jesus do. Guide them towards ideas like healing people, raising the dead and feeding hungry people.

3 Remind them that it is a good idea to spend time with God. Say that we learn more about him from the Bible. Say that the more we read the Bible, the better we will know God.

4 Encourage each child to say a prayer, asking God to do something in their life to help them to know him better.

5 Remember to ask them how God answered their prayer the next time you meet together.

Bible story picture

Why: to recognise who Jesus is
With: a copy of page 41 (also available from *LightLive*) printed on A4 paper for each child, art and craft materials

1 Remind the children that, last time, Jesus asked Peter to be his friend and Peter said 'yes'. Look at the Bible story picture and identify Jesus (on the left) and Peter. Say, 'I wonder what they are talking about...' What do the children think?

2 Listen to today's Bible story to see if you are right; then let the children complete their pictures.

3 Hold the finished pictures, look at the figure of Jesus and repeat Peter's words from Mark 8:29, 'You are the Messiah!' or say: 'Jesus is the Son of God!'

For older children

Meeting Jesus

 minutes

Why: to see how spending time with Jesus helps us to know who he is
With: books and materials to help children use their Bibles and pray

1 Ask how Jesus' friends found out who he was (by spending time with him). Say that we can do the same thing, but because Jesus now lives in heaven, we can do this by reading our Bibles (especially the bit about Jesus) and talking to Jesus in prayer.

2 You can use this opportunity to introduce materials to help children do this, such as *Massive Prayer Adventure*, *Friends Forever* and *No Girls Allowed*. If possible, show them copies to have a look through. (Visit www.scriptureunion.org.uk/shop or your local Christian bookstore for these and other publications.)

3 Encourage them to take up the challenge to pray and read the Bible more often, and to find out more about Jesus!

THE LEARN AND REMEMBER VERSE

'Come back to the LORD your God. He is kind and full of mercy; he is patient and keeps his promise; he is always ready to forgive and not punish.'

Joel 2:13b

Encourage the group to read the words together from the poster on page 59. Invite the children to define what it means to be kind, full of mercy, patient, promise-keeping, and ready to forgive. Challenge them to think of examples of when Jesus was like this.

You could also use the song 'Come back' from the *Bitesize Bible Songs* CD, available from Scripture Union.

Peter knows who Jesus is

SESSION 3
New perspective

Bible:
Mark 9:2–13

Aim: To find out that Jesus is extraordinary

CORE PROGRAMME

For 3–14s

Bible story with freeze-frames

 minutes

Why: to find out that Jesus is extraordinary
With: a digital camera or camera phone, scarf for blindfolding, SU *Bible Timeline* (all optional), sticky notes

1 Freeze-frames

In this session the children will hear and respond to sections from today's Bible story using 'freeze-frames'. A freeze-frame is a drama technique in which the children take on the role of a particular character but, instead of acting the role, they consider the facial expressions and gestures that their character might make in a certain situation and 'freeze' themselves in that particular position. This provides a good opportunity for discussion. You may also like to photograph the freeze-frames for further discussions or display purposes. (If you choose to display them, make sure you have parental consent.) After each reading, spend some time discussing possible reactions before encouraging the children to develop their own freeze-frames. Where appropriate, question some of the children about why they have chosen to take on that particular position.

2 Famous people

Tell the children about a well-known famous person (for example, the Queen) you would really like to meet. Explain how you would react if that person turned up at your front door. Ask the children who they would like to meet. What would their reaction be if their favourite sports hero knocked on their front door? Ask the children to create an individual freeze-frame to show what their reaction might be. Explain that, in today's story, Jesus takes his disciples up a mountain and there they see him meeting some famous people from Jewish history. Choose a confident reader to read Mark 9:2–6. Invite the children to tell you who the famous people were. (Moses and Elijah.)

3 Bible Timeline

Stand the children with their backs to the *Bible Timeline*. Ask for volunteers to close their eyes (or to be blindfolded) and to walk along the *Timeline*, stopping and placing a sticky note where they think Moses, Elijah and Jesus appear. Once all three sticky notes have been placed, invite the children to look and see where the people actually come. Point out that they are characters from different points in Jewish history. It was extraordinary that they would all appear in one place at the same time.

4 God's voice

Choose another confident reader to read verse 7. Ask the group who is speaking. (God) Ask how the disciples might have felt when they heard God's voice. Discuss possible responses. Draw out from them the idea that the disciples might have been shocked, but they were probably scared too. Give the children two minutes to create a freeze-frame to show the disciples' reactions.

5 Responses

Read verses 8–13. Find out from the children what happened to Moses and Elijah. (They disappeared.) How might the disciples be feeling now? (Confused, surprised.)

Give the children some time to think through the story again. Ask for a volunteer to retell the story in their own words. Then give each child a sticky note. Ask them to write or draw a question about or a response to the story, and to fix the sticky note to a wall or table.

Look at some of the responses

together. Are any of them similar? Can anyone answer any of the questions? Why do you think Jesus didn't want the disciples to tell anyone what they had seen? What does this story tell us about Jesus?

Think, write, draw

⑩ *minutes*

Why: to think of ways to describe Jesus
With: a large sheet of paper or a length of lining paper, sticky notes

1 In the middle of a large sheet of paper (or several smaller sheets stuck together), write 'Jesus' in large letters or bubble writing. Ask the children to talk about what we have learned about Jesus today.

2 Similarly, write 'Extraordinary' on the sheet of paper. Ask the children to sit quietly and think of other words that describe Jesus, and add them to the sheet. After they have thought about it and given their suggestions, give them time to draw or write what they want to say about Jesus on sticky notes, which they can stick to the sheet.

3 When they have all done this, take it in turn to thank Jesus that he is … (choose a description from the sheet).

Extraordinary reminder

⑩ *minutes*

Why: to remind the children that Jesus is extraordinary
With: plain postcards, paper

1 Remind the children that Jesus told the disciples not to say anything about what they had seen. Ask them how the disciples might have felt. Say that the mountaintop experience probably confirmed that Jesus was truly extraordinary.

2 Invite everyone, including leaders, to share an experience of Jesus being 'extraordinary'.

3 Hand out sheets of paper and postcards. Encourage the children

to make an envelope, and talk about their own extraordinary experiences with Jesus. Encourage them to write or draw an experience on a postcard to go into the envelope.

4 Pray together: 'Thank you, Jesus, that you are extraordinary! Help me to remember this when things are difficult. Amen.'

5 Tell the children to seal their envelope and keep it to open as an encouragement in difficult times.

Picture

⑧ - ⑩ *minutes*

Why: to remind us that Jesus is extraordinary
With: pieces of white card, black wax crayons, felt-tip pens, plastic spoons

1 Give each child a piece of white card and ask them to cover it with patterns using the pens. Then get them to colour over this with a black wax crayon, as thickly as possible.

2 Next, invite the children to use the end of a spoon to write the word 'Jesus' on the card by scraping off the black wax crayon. As they scrape away the crayon it should reveal their beautiful colours and patterns underneath.

3 Suggest the children take this home to remind them that Jesus is extraordinary.

EXTENSION IDEAS

Activities for younger children

Bible action rhyme

⑩ *minutes*

Why: to find out what God said about Jesus

1 Stand together, making sure the children can see the person leading the rhyme. Ask the children to join in by copying the actions of the leader. The actions are indicated in the brackets at the end of each line.

Jesus took three friends up a big hill to pray. (Walk.)

All of them were tired; they'd had a busy day. (Yawn.)

The three tired friends fell fast asleep at prayer. (Head on hands.)

Jesus prayed alone. His father God was there. (Raise hands.)

When his friends awoke, they had a great surprise. (Rub eyes.)

Jesus looked so different right before their eyes! (Gasp.)

Jesus was amazing. He stood there all in white! (Look surprised.)

He talked with God his father, shining, shining bright. (Spread arms wide.)

The friends were all amazed. Peter said, 'What shall we do?' (Shrug shoulders.)

God said, 'Listen to my Son. All his words are true.' (Cup ears.)

When the light began to fade, the friends thought of what they'd heard. (Look puzzled.)

They came down from the mountain but they dared not speak a word. (Fingers on lips.)

2 Can the children remember what the friends had heard? What did God say about Jesus? Jesus looked amazing – all shining bright. And he is amazing – because he is God's Son.

Bible story picture

Why: to realise that Jesus is extraordinary
With: a copy of page 46 (also available from *LightLive*) printed on A4 paper for each child, art and craft materials

1 Let the children colour their pictures with crayons or pencils. Say that they have coloured the pictures well – but that there is something missing. Jesus and his friends (Peter, James and John) all look near-enough the same – but the Bible story tells us that Jesus suddenly looked very different.

EXTENSION IDEAS CONTINUED

2 Look in your art and craft supplies and see what you can find to make the figure of Jesus really stand out: maybe the children could glue on glitter or sequins, or perhaps you have scraps of foil or shiny paper that could be added, or fluorescent paints or pens? Make Jesus as bright and dazzling as you can – and then see how different he looks to the other people in the picture.

For older children

Imaginative reflection

 minutes

Why: to give the young people an opportunity to spend time with Jesus in prayer
With: meditation script from page 45

1 Encourage the young people to make themselves comfortable – to find their own space, relax their bodies and close their eyes. Invite them to notice their breathing and to still themselves.

2 Slowly read the meditation, encouraging them to use their imagination and providing pauses to allow them to do so.

3 At the end, encourage everyone to become gently aware of their surroundings. Lead a prayer, thanking Jesus for meeting with you all. Remind them, if you feel it's appropriate, that it doesn't matter if they didn't 'feel' anything during the meditation – Jesus was with them.

THE LEARN AND REMEMBER VERSE

'Come back to the LORD your God. He is kind and full of mercy; he is patient and keeps his promise; he is always ready to forgive and not punish.'

Joel 2:13b

Write a few words of the verse on separate sheets of paper. Hide them prior to the session, and then invite the children to find them and put them into the correct sequence. Ask the children which words in the verse describe what Jesus was like in today's story.

Find a poster for this Learn and remember verse on page 59.

You could also use the song 'Come back' from the *Bitesize Bible Songs* CD, available from Scripture Union.

Meditation script for reflection

Read this out with some chilled-out instrumental music playing in the background.

Jesus invites you to go for a walk with him. You follow him through a beautiful wood. The sun is shining ... you can hear birds singing ... the trees provide a canopy over your head as you walk through the dappled shade of their leaves.

Slowly the ground begins to rise and you start to walk uphill. The trees thin out and now you can see the hill ahead of you. It's hard work but there's a cool breeze on your face.

Jesus is just ahead of you, not going too fast but showing you the way to go. As you climb, you think about what you know about Jesus – when you first met him, the time you have spent with him, what you think he has said to you, what other people have told you about him.

You keep climbing, steadily and rhythmically. Jesus still goes ahead, looking back and smiling at you every so often. No words are spoken, just a strong companionship as you journey together.

You keep climbing, pausing for a breath every so often, stopping to enjoy the view, continuing onwards and upwards. And then suddenly you are at the top. You stand up tall after the climb, feeling the ache in your legs and taking deep breaths of cool clean air. The view is amazing under the clear blue skies. You can see the town where you live in the distance. You know that down there everyone is hurrying around as normal amongst the noise and traffic. Up here it is completely still and quiet. But you sense that Jesus hasn't brought you up here just so you can enjoy the view. He wants to spend time with you, to show you more of who he is, to help you understand more of the mystery of God.

And so you sit down together – you are looking at Jesus, he is looking at you. No words are spoken but you can feel the warmth of his love and his presence, and your heart listens to what he has to say to you.

And you wait in the stillness, feeling safe, feeling welcome, feeling loved. You don't have to do anything or say anything or think anything – just receive the love of Jesus.

Then Jesus smiles at you. He gets up and pulls you to your feet. He puts his hand on your shoulder and looks deep into your eyes. And then he leads the way back down the hill. You follow with a deep sense of peace inside. Back down the hill with Jesus leading the way, back through the trees, back towards home. And inside, you hug the secret of this hilltop encounter as you head for home, knowing that you won't be able to put it into words, but that it is real and it will sustain you.

Shine, Jesus!

SESSION 4
Old fears

Bible:
Mark 14:27–31, 66–72

Aim: To realise that Jesus' friends sometimes get it wrong

CORE PROGRAMME

For 3–14s

Bible story with sound effects

⑮ **minutes**

Why: to realise that Jesus' friends sometimes get it wrong
With: pictures for 'Bible story with sound effects' (see page 48), SU *Bible Timeline* (optional)

1 Listen and think

Explain to the children that as Jesus' friends we sometimes make mistakes and don't treat him how we should. Ask the children to think of some of the things we might do when we are not treating Jesus as our friend. Allow time for them to share their responses. If the children are having difficulty thinking of responses, you may like to mention things such as not spending time with him, not talking to him or not treating others as he would like us to. Remind the children that, when Jesus lived on earth, sometimes his closest friends got it wrong. Tell the children that they are going to find out about Jesus' friend called Peter,

and how one day he got it wrong by not behaving like Jesus' friend.

2 *Bible Timeline*

Say that today's Bible story took place around AD 30. Challenge the children to find this date on the *Bible Timeline* and look at the paragraphs below the date to see what was going on. Draw their attention to 'Jesus on trial' and read aloud: 'Jesus was arrested and tortured. There was a trial and Jesus was sentenced to death on a cross.' Say that Peter was with Jesus when he was arrested – but then things did not go well for Peter: he let Jesus down.

3 **Prepare and practise**

Explain to the children that you are going to read the story from the Bible. During the reading they will need to make some sound effects.

Give the three pictures from page 48 to three different children. Say that everyone needs to make the sound for the picture when it is held up.

Spend some time practising the sounds for each picture. For the sheep picture say, 'Baa baa!' For the cockerel picture say, 'Cock-a-doodle-doo!' For the sad face say, 'Boo hoo!' Make sure that you give the volunteers the pictures in the right order (sheep, cockerel, sad face) and ask them to hold up the

picture each time when they hear you say the specific word ('sheep', 'cockerel' or 'rooster' and 'cried' or 'crying'). As you read the story you may need to prompt the volunteer to hold up the correct picture.

4 **Story**

Read Mark 14:27–31,66–72, with the volunteer holding up the pictures for the relevant verses: sheep, verse 27; cockerel, verse 30; cockerel, verse 68; cockerel, verse 72; sad face, end of verse 72.

5 **Reflect**

When you have finished reading the passage, hold up the picture of the sad face and ask the children why they think Peter might have cried. Challenge them to tell you how they think Jesus would have felt when Peter didn't behave as if he was his friend. Then ask, 'What about us? What things do we do that make it seem as though we aren't Jesus' friends? How does that make us feel? How does that make Jesus feel?'

Bible story with sound effects

CORE PROGRAMME CONTINUED

Prayer reminders

 minutes

Why: to know how to respond when we do wrong

1 In advance, cut bookmark shapes out of card, one for each child.

2 Tell the children that, just like Peter, we don't always treat Jesus as our friend, but we can always say sorry to him. Give each child a bookmark and ask them to draw a sad face and write 'Sorry'.

3 Invite everyone to turn their bookmarks over and say that, when we are sorry, God forgives us. Now invite the children to draw a happy face and write 'Thank you, God' next to it.

4 Encourage them to think of somewhere to put their bookmarks where they will see them. Tell them that the bookmark reminds us to treat Jesus as our friend. Assure them that even if we get things wrong, as Peter did, Jesus forgives us if we are sorry.

Discussion and game

 minutes

Why: to affirm or reaffirm our commitment to following Jesus

1 Invite the children to suggest ways in which we may fail Jesus. (Perhaps by not admitting that we are Christians or by not standing up for someone who is being bullied.)

2 Say that a few sessions ago we learned about when Peter decided to follow Jesus (read Mark 1:16–18). Ask the children whether they have ever decided to follow Jesus. (Don't demand a response, but encourage them to chat with you afterwards if they have considered making such a decision or want to today.)

3 Invite the children to play 'Follow the leader', changing leaders every round. Tell the leader to shout out a phrase of commitment (for example, 'I will always follow Jesus!') and

invite the followers to repeat this phrase while imitating the leader's actions.

Game

 *minutes*

Why: to review key incidents in Peter's life
With: notes of key events in Peter's life (see page 51)

1 Tell the children that you will describe some events in Peter's life. Ask them to crow whenever you mention something that Peter does that is wrong or foolish. However, whenever they think Peter acts correctly or wisely, they must clap. Use the notes from page 51 or these Bible passages:

- Mark 1:16–18; 14:32–42;
- Luke 5:1–11;
- Matthew 14:25–29,30; 16:15–23;
- John 6:66–69; 18:10,11;
- Acts 2:14; 4:15–20.

2 To make it more challenging, read out each Bible reference, asking the children to look them up and respond accordingly.

EXTENSION IDEAS

Activities for younger children

Biscuit faces

 minutes

Why: to think about our response to not treating Jesus as our friend
With: plain biscuits, icing, decorations such as liquorice laces and jelly sweets, plates, plastic knives

1 Make sure the children wash their hands before they start this activity and be aware of allergies!

2 Remind the children of Peter's response when he realised he did not act like Jesus' friend. Encourage them to use the icing and decorations to make a sad face on a biscuit. Ask the children to look at the sad face biscuit and say sorry

to Jesus for the times they haven't treated him like a friend.

3 Explain that the happy news is that, if we tell Jesus we are sorry, he promises to forgive us. Invite them to make a happy face on another biscuit to remind them of God's forgiveness.

Bible story picture

Why: to discover that being a friend of Jesus is not always easy
With: a copy of page 52 (also available from *LightLive*) printed on A4 paper for each child, art and craft materials

1 Help the children to identify Peter on the Bible story picture. Remind them that you have had other pictures of Peter in your Bible stories. Peter became a friend of Jesus; Peter knew Jesus was the Son of God; Peter saw Jesus bright and dazzling with the amazingness of God. But this picture only shows Peter and not Jesus. Where is Jesus? (He has been taken away by the soldiers.)

2 Can the children find a cockerel in the picture? See if any of them can tell the others what a cockerel is – and demonstrate what noise it makes. It looks as though the bird in the picture is making a noise like that! But why is Peter looking so worried? Listen to the Bible story to find out.

For older children

Discussion and Bible study

 *minutes*

Why: to see that we sometimes get it wrong
With: Bibles

1 Ask the young people: 'What is the worst thing you have ever done to a friend?' Encourage them to share their stories, being sensitive to the fact that some of them may find this difficult.

2 Lead a discussion on their stories using the following questions:

EXTENSION IDEAS CONTINUED

- How did you feel afterwards?
- How did your behaviour affect the friendship?
- How would you do things differently if you had the chance?

3 Hand out Bibles. Explain that Peter had a best friend for whom he would have done anything. Get everyone to find Mark 14:27–31 and follow as you read. Say that Peter wanted to do the right thing, but when the time came he let Jesus down. Read Mark 14:66–72.

4 Ask your group to think about how Peter's friendship with Jesus might have been affected by this. Get them to share their thoughts.

5 Explain that Peter was one of Jesus' disciples and is one of the most famous Christians to have ever lived. In fact, he was instrumental in building the church, and yet even he got things wrong here.

THE LEARN AND REMEMBER VERSE

'Come back to the LORD your God. He is kind and full of mercy; he is patient and keeps his promise; he is always ready to forgive and not punish.'

Joel 2:13b

Ask the children to make placards relating to today's verse, each containing an adjective or phrase describing God (kind, full of mercy). Read the verse, pausing for everyone to shout out the appropriate attribute while waving their placards. Discuss what each one means.

Find a poster for this Learn and remember verse on page 59.

You could also use the song 'Come back' from the *Bitesize Bible Songs* CD, available from Scripture Union.

Events for 'Game'

Mark 1:16–18
Jesus invites Simon (Peter) and Andrew to follow him – at once, they leave their boats behind and follow Jesus.

Luke 5:1-5
Jesus tells Simon (Peter) to let down his nets in deep water – and he does!

Luke 5:8
Peter tells Jesus not to come near him because he is a sinner.

Matthew 14:25–29
Peter walks on water.

Matthew 14:30
Peter begins to sink.

Matthew 16:15–20
Peter responds to Jesus' question, 'Who do you say that I am?'

Matthew 16:21–23
Peter tries to persuade Jesus not to go to Jerusalem.

John 6:66–69
Jesus asks his disciples whether they are going to leave him, and Peter replies, 'Lord, there's no one else that we can go to! Your words give eternal life...'

John 18:10,11
Peter cuts off the ear of the high priest's servant.

Mark 14:32–42
Jesus tells his disciples to stay awake and pray; Peter falls asleep.

Acts 2:14
Peter preaches boldly at Pentecost.

Acts 4:15–20
Peter is warned not to preach about Jesus, but he refuses.

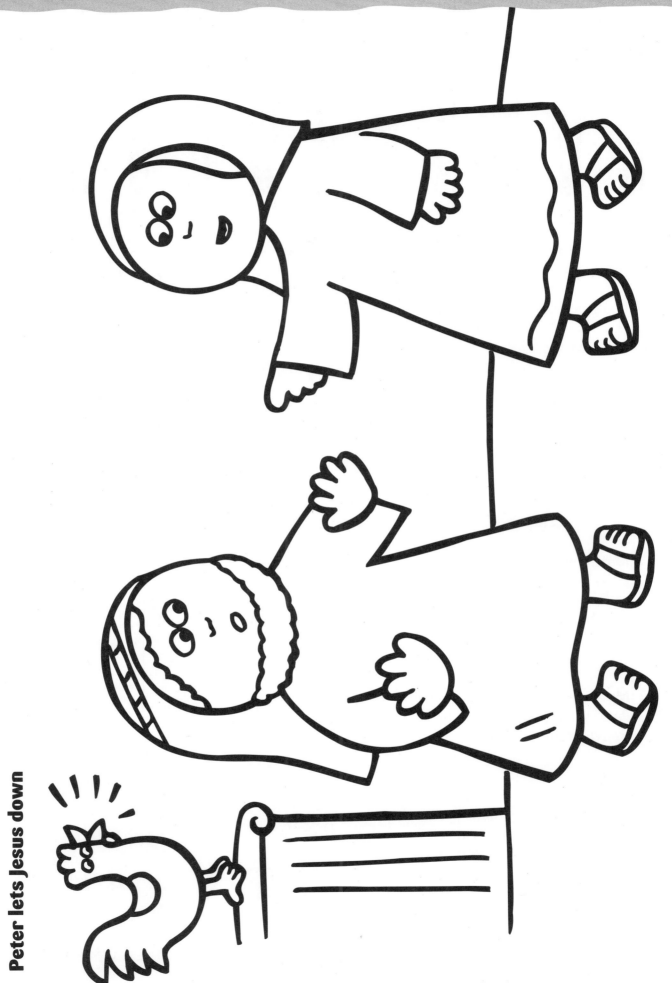

Peter lets Jesus down

SESSION 5
New start

Bible:
John 21:15–19

Aim: To discover that Jesus welcomes us back

CORE PROGRAMME

For 3–14s

Interactive Bible story

⑮ – ⑳ *minutes*

Why: to discover that Jesus welcomes us back
With: a portable barbecue (optional), fish and bread (or an alternative), a costume for Peter (optional), SU *Bible Timeline*

1 **Travel back in time**
Tell the children that today's story happened a long time ago when some people were eating fish on a beach, and that's what they're going to do today! Aim to recreate a scene similar to that in John 21:9 where Jesus prepared a breakfast of bread and fish for the disciples. It would be great if you could go outside or try to recreate a beach scene indoors. The more dramatic your introduction, the more the children will remember it! Serve some food to all the children (tuna sandwiches if hot food is not feasible), give thanks and enjoy eating together.

There are obvious health and safety issues here. Check for allergies and diet preferences and ensure you have adequate adult supervision and clear boundaries in place, particularly if you decide to use a barbecue outside.

2 **Peter's story**
Ask another adult to prepare this script or to tell Peter's story in their own words:

Mmm. That fish smells delicious! It reminds me of… Oh, hello everyone! My name's Peter. Enjoying your barbecue? I was just saying it reminds me of a time when I was on the beach with Jesus. It happened after Jesus came back to life.

I did not think Jesus would want me to be his friend any more. When Jesus was arrested, I was waiting outside and someone asked me if I was with Jesus. I was afraid I'd be arrested, too. I let Jesus down. I said I didn't know him. Not once, but three times! I felt dreadful! I cried. I thought Jesus would never trust me again.

Then Jesus died and rose from the dead, just as he promised – but I didn't think he would want to know me any more. I went back to my old job, fishing. One night we caught nothing.

Someone told us to cast our nets on the other side of the boat. We brought them up full of fish! We didn't realise it was Jesus at first, but it was! He cooked us breakfast too.

After we'd eaten, Jesus asked me if I loved him. Three times he asked – just like the three times I said I didn't know him. Jesus asked me to care for his sheep. I couldn't believe it – Jesus was actually welcoming me back! He knew I was sorry for letting him down and he still wanted to be my friend. He gave me a special job – to look after his followers. That's what he meant by caring for his sheep. It felt so good to know Jesus understood and loved me and welcomed me back! I cried again, but this time they were tears of joy, not sadness.

3 **Think and chat**
Ask the children to work in pairs and talk about these questions:

- Who was Peter?
- What had he done?
- What did Jesus do?
- How did Peter feel?

Look at the *Bible Timeline* together and find where this story fits in (just before Jesus goes to heaven). Explain that, although Peter lived a long time ago, Jesus is still the same today. Any time we let him down

CORE PROGRAMME CONTINUED

(and we all do), he knows how we feel. When we're sorry, he forgives us and welcomes us back, just like he did Peter. See if the children can spot Peter's name further along the *Bible Timeline*. Chat about what Peter did after Jesus went back to heaven.

4 Pray

Encourage the children to pray short sentences of response to the story. You could use the abbreviation TSP to structure the prayers, saying, 'Thanks', then 'Sorry' and finally 'Please'.

Response with actions

 minutes

Why: to remember that Jesus died to welcome us into God's kingdom

1 Teach the children these actions for the following commands:

- **Reach down** – stand straight, bend low, touch toes;
- **Reach up** – lift arms straight above head;
- **Reach in** – cross arms over chest;
- **Reach out** – spread arms wide.

2 Say:

God reached down to us by sending Jesus.

We reach up to God in prayer and receive forgiveness.

The Holy Spirit in us helps us to obey God.

We reach out and share God's love with others.

3 Invite the children to repeat the actions slowly, while thanking Jesus for forgiving them and welcoming them back.

Creative prayer

 **minutes**

Why: to illustrate that Jesus welcomes us back
With: some blank index cards

1 Give each child an index card. Tell them to write the Learn and remember verse (Joel 2:13b) on one side and the words 'Welcome back' in large letters on the other side. Get them to cover the welcome side with a sticky note.

2 Invite the children to write some of the wrong things they have done on their sticky note (assure them that no one will see these).

3 Encourage the children to silently pray and ask God to forgive them. Then invite them to peel off the note and crumple or tear it up. Say that when we tell Jesus we are sorry, he forgives us and welcomes us back!

4 Encourage them to take their card home to remind them that God forgives us.

Make and pray

⑩ **minutes**

Why: to remember that Jesus welcomes us back
With: prayer strips for 'Make and pray' (see page 56), coloured paper, party poppers, music (optional)

1 In advance, copy the prayer strips for 'Make and pray' (page 56) onto coloured paper and cut into strips. Cut extra strips of blank coloured paper.

2 Read aloud Jesus' words from Luke 15:7 (CEV). Encourage the children to imagine the angels rejoicing when we say sorry to Jesus and are welcomed back. Perhaps it's like a welcome back party!

3 Ask the children to choose a prayer they would like to say to God from the strips. They could also write their own short prayers on a blank strip. Use these and extra strips to make paper chains, and hang them up in the room.

4 Have a welcome back party. Use party poppers (safely); play party music and simple games like musical bumps.

EXTENSION IDEAS
Activities for younger children

Role play

⑩ **minutes**

Why: to practise welcoming back, as Jesus did
With: scenario cards for 'Role play' (see page 58) (optional)

1 Explain that people who love and follow Jesus try to live like he did. Talk about how hard it is to welcome others back when they have done something to hurt us.

2 Get the children into small groups of two or three, each with a scenario card. Ask them to act out what Jesus would want them to do and say in the situations depicted on the cards: Your sister breaks your favourite toy; Your baby brother chews up the great picture you have just done; Your best friend doesn't invite you to her birthday but later says sorry.

3 Invite each group, in turn, to tell everyone what was on their card and show their response to it. Commend each group after their presentation.

Bible story picture

Why: to know that Jesus forgives
With: a copy of page 58 (also available from *LightLive*) printed on A4 paper for each child, art and craft materials

1 Look at the Bible-story picture and identify Jesus (on the left) and Peter. Say, 'I wonder what they are talking about...' What do the children think?

2 Remind them that Peter had let Jesus down. Peter said he was not a friend of Jesus – but look again at the picture. Do they look friendly here? Agree that they do and show that you are pleased that they are friends again. But what can have happened?

3 Read the Bible story or tell it in your own words, while the children complete their pictures.

For older children

Meditation and prayer

 minutes

Why: to enable the young people to respond to Jesus' question, 'Do you love me?'

With: Bible, instrumental music, CD or MP3 player with speakers

1 Get a leader to read John 21:15–17 and then explain that you are going to read the passage out again, but this time you want the young people to imagine that it is them on the beach with Jesus, not Peter. They don't have to do or say anything out loud, but just imagine their responses in their heads.

2 Encourage everyone to relax, get into a comfortable position and close their eyes. Then start the instrumental music quietly.

3 Get a leader to read out John 21:15–17 slowly. Instead of reading Peter's replies, ask, 'How are you going to answer Jesus?' and pause for a while. Instead of reading 'Feed my lambs', 'Take care of my sheep' and 'Feed my sheep', ask, 'What does that mean for you?' and again pause for a while.

4 Finish with a simple prayer receiving God's forgiveness, such as: 'Loving Lord, thank you that you offer each one of us your forgiveness and a chance to start again. Help us to accept that forgiveness through Jesus Christ, our Lord. Amen.'

THE LEARN AND REMEMBER VERSE

'Come back to the Lord your God. He is kind and full of mercy; he is patient and keeps his promise; he is always ready to forgive and not punish.'

Joel 2:13b

Read the words of the Learn and remember verse and ask the group to pick out the words that show what God is like. These words (kind, full of mercy, patient and so on) are why God wants to welcome us back when we have done wrong. Invite the children to suggest an incident from Jesus' life (something he did or a story he told) that illustrates God's readiness to welcome us back. Thank God together for his readiness to welcome us back despite the wrong things we do.

Find a poster for this Learn and remember verse on page 59.

You could also use the song 'Come back' from the *Bitesize Bible Songs* CD, available from Scripture Union.

Make and pray prayer strips

Thank you, Jesus, that you welcome me back.

Jesus, I want to be your friend.

Jesus, you are a really great friend.

Jesus, thank you for welcoming Peter back.

Role play scenario cards

A

Your sister breaks your favourite toy. She comes to say sorry. What do you say?

B

Your baby brother chews up the great picture you have just done. He doesn't understand why you are upset. What do you do?

C

Your best friend doesn't invite you to her birthday. Later she says sorry and asks if you can still be friends. What do you say?

Peter and Jesus are friends

'Come back to the LORD your God. He is kind and full of mercy; he is patient and keeps his promise; he is always ready to forgive and not punish.'

Joel 2:13b

ALL-AGE SERVICE
Peter – this is your life!

Readings:
Mark 1:16–20; John 21:15–19; Joel 2:12,13

Aim: to review Peter's life up to when he met Jesus after the resurrection, and to identify what it means for us to live with Jesus

GETTING STARTED

In this service, we will focus on Peter and how we are like or unlike him, and also see what it means to live with Jesus.

Living with Jesus is both wonderful and difficult. It is not easy for us, just as it was not easy for those who shared Jesus' earthly life. There are ups and downs in our perceptions and experiences of Jesus, because we are inconstant human beings. Sometimes we have moments of illumination – but sometimes we fail to follow him, in small ways or, sometimes, spectacularly.

Yet Jesus entrusted the church to Peter, however flawed and human he was. Jesus forgave him, reinstated him, restored him and empowered him. He does all those things for us, too, so no matter how feeble we feel or how many mistakes we make, our connection with Jesus is always renewable and the invitation to live with him is a permanent one.

YOU WILL NEED

- PETER written vertically on two sheets of a flip chart; pen
- a CD player, if learning the Learn and remember verse with the CD version – see Music and song ideas
- script for interview with Peter and an interviewee; big, red 'This is your life' book for the **Bible talk** (optional)
- a timeline for everyone (see page 64); pens and pencils for the **Prayer activity**

BEGINNING THE SERVICE

Explain that this service is going to be focused around the life of Peter, whom the children will have encountered in their groups. Show the five letters that spell his name and ask for words or phrases beginning with these four letters that describe Peter. These might include: pushy, puts his foot in it, practical, extrovert, energetic, enthusiastic, ebullient, terrified, talented, reckless, rushed, rough, rude.

Then explain that you have all come to worship God. What words or phrases can you think of that describe God, using these same four letters? These might include: powerful, present, people-loving, everywhere, energetic, everlasting, tower of strength, trustworthy, truthful, right, righteous, ruler, reigning.

Include as many of these words as you can in an introductory prayer, followed by songs of worship and praise to God.

BIBLE READING

During the Bible talk, several passages from Mark and John will be read. Make sure that the person who reads them has practised and reads with clarity and warmth.

The Learn and remember verse for this series is Joel 2:13b which in the GNB reads: 'Come back to the LORD your God. He is kind and full of mercy; he is patient and keeps his promise; he is always ready to forgive and not punish.' This is available in a song version as 'Come back' on the *Bitesize Bible Songs* CD (SU).

Learn the verse (and the song if appropriate), commenting that the prophet Joel probably delivered this message to the people of God when they were living in exile. God called the people back to himself and offered them hope. Peter made all kinds of mistakes, but Jesus restored him and gave him hope. If the children already know the song, invite them to lead the singing.

BIBLE TALK

With: an actor playing Peter; someone who has agreed to answer the same questions as Peter's about their own life; a prepared person to read the Bible; a big, red 'This is your life' book (optional)

First, carry out an interview with the adult who will give their personal testimony, using the 'This is your life' book if appropriate.

■ Why did you think it was worth following Jesus? (Answer focuses on what the person found interesting about Jesus. They should not talk about the influence of other people.)

■ But there's more to Jesus than that, isn't there? Was there one time when you realised who he really was or was it a more gradual process? (Answer should either focus on a spiritual revelation when 'the penny dropped' or acknowledge that realising who Jesus is can often happen over a period of time. Whatever response you get, assure everyone that we all come to Jesus in our own unique way. We are all different.)

■ Have you ever felt stunned by an experience of living with Jesus? (Answer should focus on an unusual event which was awe-inspiring, perhaps unnerving.)

■ Would you say you were a good friend to Jesus? (Answer in terms of 'could do better', mentioning failings, but acknowledging that he goes on loving us and being our friend.)

Then ask these same questions of the actor playing Peter, using the 'This is your life' book if you have one.

■ Why did you think it was worth following Jesus? (Peter tells the story from John 1:35–42 and then says, 'Listen to how my friend John Mark writes about it. He kept a close account of what Jesus said and did. It's in his Gospel.' Read out Mark 1:16–18.)

■ But there's more to Jesus than that, isn't there? Was there a time when you realised who Jesus really was? (Peter tells how he had several experiences when things became clearer, but then explain in more detail the story of the transfiguration from Mark 9:2–13. Peter concludes by referring to the statement he made about Jesus just before this happened. Peter says, 'Listen to how my friend John Mark writes about it. It's in his Gospel.' Read Mark 8:27–30.)

■ Would you say you were a good friend to Jesus? (Peter talks about being one of the closest three disciples to Jesus, witnessing the transfiguration. But, he deserted Jesus at the arrest in the garden. Peter begins to tell the story of his denial of Jesus, which was when he realised what a poor friend he was – but says, 'Listen to how my friend John Mark writes about it. It's in his Gospel.' Read Mark 14:66–72.)

■ Have you ever felt stunned by an experience of living with Jesus? (Peter tells the story of his meeting on the beach with Jesus after the resurrection from John 21:1–14. After this, Peter knew he was forgiven and had a role to play in spreading the good news of Jesus. Read John 21:15–17.)

Conclude by saying that Peter was to learn what it meant to live for Jesus. Open the 'This is your life' book and ask, rhetorically, what people would want to put in this book about their own life with Jesus. You will need to explain the 'This is your life' concept which may not be known by younger people! (If appropriate, you could ask people to break into groups to talk about this.) Comment that we all let Jesus down, just as Peter did. But just like him, we can also be forgiven, making a fresh start. This is what life with Jesus means.

Sing or say the Learn and remember verse again.

PRAYER ACTIVITY

With: a simple timeline for everyone (see page 64); pens and pencils

This should follow on directly from the Bible talk. Give everyone a timeline which is marked as follows, working left to right:

■ date of birth;
■ a time when I knew Jesus loved me;
■ a time when I knew Jesus had forgiven me;
■ a time when I said or did something to help others hear about Jesus.

Emphasise that we can all come to Jesus in different ways – some people may not be sure yet whether they know his love and forgiveness.

Ask everyone to complete the timeline for themselves, writing or drawing symbols of the significant times. You could show how it works by completing your own timeline for everyone to see or by doing one for the person who was interviewed. Conclude by giving time for everyone to talk with Jesus, thanking him that he is our friend and never gives up on us.

Alternatively, you could make mini-red books for everyone labelled 'This is your life' and invite people to write something in their book and then talk with God about what they have written. They could take the book home or do this as an Ending the service activity.

PRAYER OF CONFESSION

Peter let Jesus down. And he was deeply sorry about this. He needed to be forgiven so he could go on living with Jesus.

Jesus Christ, there have been times this week when we have said things which a friend of yours should not say. *(Pause)*

Please forgive us.

Jesus Christ, there have been times this week when we have done things which a friend of yours should not do. *(Pause)*

Please forgive us.

Jesus Christ, there have been times when we have pretended that we are not your friend, when we have not loved you and when we have not enjoyed your company. *(Pause)*

Please forgive us.

Jesus forgave Peter and gave him an important task to do. He promises to forgive all those who admit they have done wrong and want to put things right. His Spirit enables us to live for Jesus.

Day by day, O Lord, three things I pray:

■ to see thee more clearly;
■ to love thee more dearly;
■ to follow thee more nearly, day by day.

Amen

A prayer of Richard of Chichester (1197–1253)

PRAYERS OF INTERCESSION

It would be appropriate to pray for any activities that are occurring now or in the near future that are seeking to introduce people to Jesus and so become his friend. This might include a holiday club, Christian holiday activity or an Alpha-type course. It is an opportunity to pass on information and encourage prayer by the whole church.

It might be appropriate to prepare a bookmark (or mini-red book) to give to everyone before the prayer time for them to take home.

ENDING THE SERVICE

With: PETER written vertically on a flip chart (see Beginning the service); pen

So, how can we live with Jesus, this week? Ask for words or phrases that begin with the letters of Peter's name. These might include: pray, persevere, patient, energetic, explain about Jesus, exceptionally helpful, expectant of God, truthful, trusting, talking to lonely people, reassuring, reading the Bible, reflecting on Jesus.

HELPFUL EXTRAS

Music and song ideas

- 'All that I am, all that I do' (*Songs of Fellowship* 647);
- 'O Jesus, I have promised' (*SOF* 418);
- 'Jesus put this song into our hearts' (*SOF* 299);
- 'Purify my heart' (*SOF* 475):
- 'Lord of all hopefulness' (*SOF* 902);
- 'Dear Lord and Father of mankind' (*SOF* 79);
- 'I reach up high' (*SOF* 1358);
- 'Come back' (*Bitesize Bible Songs* CD, available from Scripture Union) – the Learn and remember verse for Joel 2:13b;
- 'God is an awesome God' (*LFE*);
- 'When you make a mistake' (*RU*)

NOTES AND COMMENTS

To help you explain what it means to be a follower of Jesus, get hold of a copy of *Top Tips on Helping a child respond to Jesus* (see page 31 for more details).

In this service there is a challenge to everyone to consider how they have responded to Jesus, both now and in the past. Younger children may not be able to articulate it clearly (but that is true for many adults too). Try to present a clear and sensitive challenge to everyone to go on living with Jesus from this point on. You will want to have some literature to pass on to anyone who wants to know more. *Jesus=friendship forever*, *Me+Jesus* and *Friends with Jesus* are three Scripture Union booklets you would want to use with under 12s.

There are many more resources, based on episodes from Peter's life, available from SU, including the Scripture Union holiday club programmes, *Seaside Rock* and *Rocky's Plaice* (with accompanying DVDs), *Take Away* (an eyelevel midweek club programme) and the children's book, *Peter puts his foot in it*.

For more details visit:
www.scriptureunion.org.uk

My timeline

Date of birth.	A time when I knew Jesus loved me.	A time when I knew Jesus had forgiven me.	A time when I said or did something to help others hear about Jesus.

My timeline

Date of birth.	A time when I knew Jesus loved me.	A time when I knew Jesus had forgiven me.	A time when I said or did something to help others hear about Jesus.

Mosaic clinic

Top tips from ministry practitioners to help you make the most of your small group with a wide age range

Nobody denies that working with a few children with a wide age range presents challenges! However, help is at hand... Here are a few ideas which might make the work easier and more enjoyable for everyone.

Encourage the older children and the younger ones

It's very tempting – and very easy – with a small group and a wide age range to simply pitch everything in the middle. But if you think back to the idea of the group as a 'family' rather than a 'class', that would be like everyone having to always do, eat and watch what the 8-year-old wants!

Encourage the older children to help you set up and run the group, and to mentor the younger ones. This is not a skill that comes naturally to most young people but, in the context of a small group, you have time to train the older children in coaching the younger ones. It's a good environment in which to build confidence – the older child leading the younger; the younger trusting the older ones. But...

Have activities that respect older children

Older children and young people are not spare helpers! They are not there just to help out or make your task easier. Make sure they have activities that respect their age and which enable them to grow in faith too.

But at the same time, you can help them to take real responsibility. You have time to take a risk on them and demonstrate your trust in them. Ask them to prepare the prayers for next time; or to book the projector and get it set up.

In reality...

> *AT MY CHURCH, WE USED TO HAVE AN 11-YEAR-OLD LAD RUNNING THE POWERPOINT THROUGH THE MORNING SERVICE – HE WAS GREAT – MUCH BETTER THAN THE ADULTS WHO DO IT NOW!*

Give them real tasks to do that will challenge and stretch them – and be ready to pick up the pieces and give them another chance, if necessary.

Be aware of the needs of younger children

As you need at least two adults with the group, consider making one leader responsible for helping the younger children.

They are physically smaller and uncoordinated; their language and understanding is developing and they are still dependent on adults in many ways, so think about how they can be included, whilst taking account of their age and abilities. Choose games where they will not get squashed, and art activities that allow the children to be expressive without needing a certain answer. When you're planning stories or drama, remember that they believe what they're told and take everything literally, so be careful and accurate.

Think about...

> *HOW MIGHT YOU HANDLE A TELLING OF THE PARABLE OF THE LOST SHEEP, FOR INSTANCE?*

ELISHA THE PROPHET

*Be confident in God's power
and learn to trust him*

BIBLE BACKGROUND FOR YOU

**Elisha's request when Elijah departed
was for a double portion of the Spirit that
had empowered Elijah. His request was
granted as he saw Elijah leave – and here
we see him acting with God's power.**

The first two accounts are very similar to
events in the life of Elijah. God provides and
God gives life. The story of Naaman acts as
a further reminder of God's power to heal,
but it also shows that God acts outside the
boundaries of Israel. God's power is not
limited – nor is the scope of his love.

The final story is a powerful one, showing God
at work in the military and political realms. It
opens our eyes (as well as those of Elisha's
servant) to the intimate connection between
the physical and the spiritual. We can limit
God's power to the spiritual realm, forgetting
that he is also interested in the way in which
we run our societies – military matters and
political issues are as much his concern as
what we do in church on Sunday. How active
are we in the affairs of our community? How
often do we pray about political issues? By
contrast, however, we can also become too
tied in to the physical world, losing sight of
spiritual realities. Most people around us are
only aware of the physical and are sceptical
of the spiritual. And where they become
interested in the spiritual it is often unbalanced
and lacks any reference to God. How can we
help them to a better understanding?

For your small group with a wide age range

God's power is the focus of this series
about Elisha. We will see God providing
for a family, raising a child from death,
healing a soldier and defeating an army.
Most of these stories have a strange
ring nowadays, but the message of
God's intervention in human affairs is
just as relevant. Encourage the group,
however small it is, to be confident in
God and to trust him. We may be few
and weak, but he is powerful. Be sure
to note that God uses his power for
positive purposes. When we pray, we
ask him to do good, loving things.

Resources for ministry

*The Big Bible
Storybook*
contains 188
Bible stories
told for under-
5s, including
the four
stories about
Elisha in this
series. Plus colour
pictures for each story to explore
and discuss with the youngest in
your group.

Highlights from *LightLive*

Go to the 'Search *LightLive*' tab at
www.lightlive.org and enter this
session's Bible reference to find:

- 'Bible story picture': a regular
  activity for 2–7s
- 'Audio Bible story': a regular
  mp3 download for 3–7s
- 'Learn and remember': a
  PowerPoint of a Bible verse
  to learn, for 5–11s (see also page
  95)
- 'Presentation': an activity with
  animation for 11–14s

SESSION 1

Powerful provider

Bible:
2 Kings 4:1–7

Aim: To explore how God provides for his people through his power

CORE PROGRAMME

For 3–14s

Bible story with props

 20 *minutes*

Why: to explore how God provides through his power
With: a small jar, a large jug of water, containers, modelling clay (optional), SU *Bible Timeline*

1 Prepare

If you are able to, ask the children each to bring in two or three containers (such as empty yogurt pots, plastic bowls, empty jars or plastic cups) for this session. Alternatively, you could bring in enough yourself.

2 Set up

Make sure everyone has at least one container and give out the modelling clay. Ask the children to make bowls with it. Choose leaders or children to play the woman and her sons, and ask the rest of the group to sit around the room, with their bowls.

3 Tell the story

Read the story as follows:

One day a woman came to Elisha to tell him that her husband had died. She told Elisha that her husband had loved God, but he had owed some money when he died. Now the person who was owed the money was demanding it back. If she didn't pay, he said he would take her two sons as his slaves.

Elisha asked, 'How much food do you have in the house?'

'Nothing at all, except a small jar of olive oil,' she replied. (*Invite the 'woman' to hold up the small jar.*)

'Then borrow as many pots and pans as you can from all your friends and neighbours,' he instructed.

(*Encourage the 'woman' and her 'sons' to collect containers from the other children.*)

Elisha told her, 'Go into your house with your sons and shut the door behind you. Then pour olive oil from your jar into the pots and pans, setting them aside as they are filled.'

(*Ask the children what they think is going to happen when the woman pours the oil into the pots and pans. Then ask the 'woman' to tip up her small jar and pretend to fill the first pot. As she does, get a leader to pour water from the big jug so that the pot becomes full. Invite the 'sons' to remove the full pots and pass the empty ones across until all the pots are full.*)

So she did. Her sons brought the pots and pans to her and she filled one after another! Soon every container was full to the brim.

'Bring me another jar,' she said to her sons.

'There aren't any more,' they told her, and the oil stopped flowing.

When she told the prophet what had happened, he said to her, 'Go and sell the oil and pay off your debt and there will be enough money left for you and your sons to live on.'

That's what she did. And that's what happened.

4 Chat

Tell the children that God often uses ordinary people (like us) when he does powerful miracles in someone else's life. In this story God used Elisha, the woman and her neighbours too.

Ask the children how they think God could use them.

Now look at the *Bible Timeline* and see if the children can identify other people whom God has used to show his power. Emphasise that people don't do miracles – God does. He just chooses to use people! Encourage the children to think about ways in which God might use them to help other people.

Touch, taste, see

⑮ minutes

Why: to introduce 'oil'
With: samples of oil, paper towels, soap

1 Collect together a selection of oils from everyday life, such as engine oil, 3-in-One oil (sometimes called 'sewing machine oil'), vegetable oil, olive oil, aromatherapy oils, cod liver oil and anything else you have or can borrow. Make sure you have paper towels and washing facilities.

2 Give the young people a chance to touch and feel the different oils, and to taste the appropriate ones. (Be aware of allergies here.)

3 Discuss how important oil is for everyday life – not just the carbon-based one which we use for fuel, but also the olive, vegetable and soya oils used in cooking.

4 Invite the group to think about which oil is the most important and to say why.

5 If appropriate, say that in homes in Old Testament times, a jar of oil would always have been available. However, oil by itself is of little use.

Physical praise

⑤ minutes

Why: to recognise God's provision

1 Ask the children to find a space. Explain that you will say a time of day (for example, 'morning') and that they should call out things that God provides at that time of day, such as 'energy', 'water for washing' or 'breakfast'.

2 As the children call out their ideas, encourage them to do an appropriate action. For instance, for 'energy' they could run on the spot.

3 Finish with a praise shout: 'Thank you, God, for providing for us every morning!'

4 Repeat the activity using other times of day.

Research and plan

⑩ minutes

Why: to think about how we can be part of God's way to provide
With: suggested websites (see below)

1 Invite the children to look at the information. If it is about a charity that you support already, encourage the children to share what they know about it.

2 Ask: 'What needs do these people have? How might God provide for them?' Hopefully the children will suggest raising money to help. Choose one of the charities and make a plan together to raise some money by, for example, a cake sale or a concert.

3 Explain that we can help provide for others, but it is God's work so we need his help, too. Pray together, thanking God for his power to provide and asking for his blessing on the plans you have made.

Look at the following websites to help you search for a particular organisation that your group might try to support. Print off some photos or information that the children could use in their research.

- www.worldvision.org.uk
- www.savethechildren.org.uk
- www.nspcc.org.uk
- www.toyboxcharity.org.uk
- www.standupforkids.org

EXTENSION IDEAS

Activities for younger children

Snap game

 minutes

Why: to think about how God wants us all to have enough
With: copies of page 70 on card, scissors, crayons

1 Make at least one copy of page 70 per child. Cut the pictures out to make a set of playing cards.

2 Mix the cards up and give each child an equal number. Play 'Snap' with the cards in one big group, or a few smaller groups. Keep playing until one or two children have most of the cards. What does it feel like to have hardly any? This might be how the woman felt with only a bit of oil. What does it feel like to have lots of cards? That might be how the woman felt when she had lots of oil.

3 God cares for poor people and he wants us all to have enough. Gather all the cards and spread them out, showing the pictures. Let the children sort out one of each picture, to colour and keep.

Bible story picture

Why: to find out that God cares about people who are poor
With: a copy of page 72 (also available from *LightLive*) printed on A4 paper for each child, art and craft materials

1 Look at the Bible story picture and count how many people you can see. Explain that these people are a family: a mum and her two sons.

2 See if the children can count the pots and jars in the picture: how many are there? The pots were empty, but now the mum is pouring something into them: what could it be? Explain that the tiny jar in her hand has oil in it – and she is going to fill all those big jars with oil from just that little jar. Act puzzled about this: how could it happen? There are lots of big jars and not much oil in that one little jar.

3 Say that one person is missing from the picture. One of God's messengers, Elisha, told the woman what to do. And Elisha knew because God told him. Find out what happened with today's Bible story.

For older children

Chat

 minutes

Why: to see that ultimately God provides everything
With: pictures from page 71

1 Give out copies of page 71. If there are enough children, encourage them to work in pairs.

2 Invite the children to look at the pictures and discuss how God provides each of the items pictured. This is quite obscure for some of the items, such as the television! (God created electricity and gives people the ability to invent and act.)

3 After a few minutes, bring the group together to share their answers. Emphasise that, ultimately, God provides everything.

THE LEARN AND REMEMBER VERSE

'I know, LORD, that you are all-powerful; that you can do everything you want.'

Job 42:2

Write the verse in the centre of a large sheet of paper. Around the edge, invite the children to draw pictures of things that God does through his power. These can be examples from nature or from Bible stories. Read the verse together several times.

Find a poster for this Learn and remember verse on page 95.

Alternatively, use the song 'Everything you want' on the *Bitesize Bible Songs 2* CD, available from Scripture Union.

Snap cards

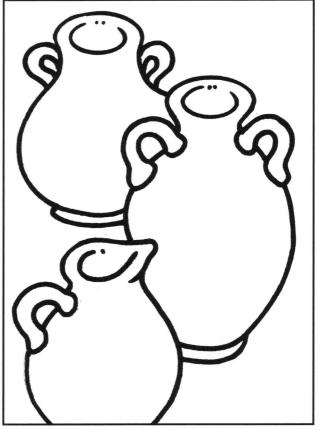
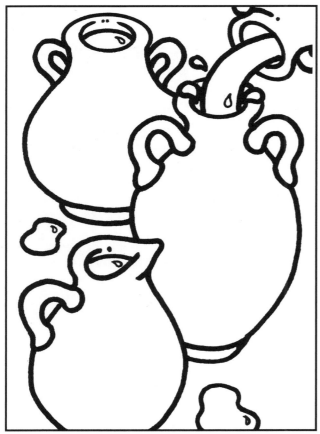

Chat

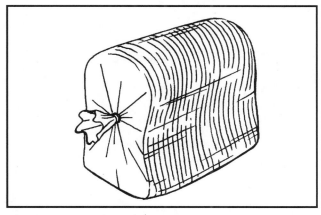

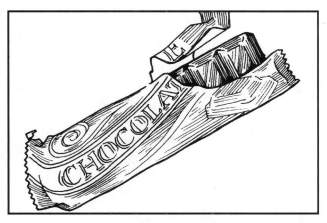
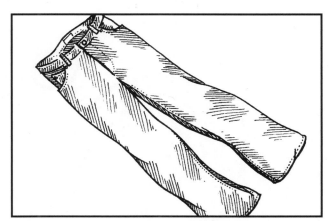

Elisha helps a family

SERIES 3 ELISHA THE PROPHET
SESSION 2
Powerful life-giver

Bible:
2 Kings 4:8–37

Aim: To trust God because he is the powerful life-giver

CORE PROGRAMME
For 3–14s

Bible story with model

⑳ *minutes*

Why: to trust God because he is the powerful life-giver
With: SU *Bible Timeline* (optional), a shoebox or similar, reusable sticky tack, a matchbox or similar, pictures for 'Bible story with model' from page 74 (optional)

1 **Guess the character**
Explain to the children that you are going to pretend to be a character on the SU *Bible Timeline* and they have to guess who you are. Say some sentences as if you were Adam, for example, 'I lived in a garden. I was the first man God made.' Follow thereafter with Eve, then Daniel and then Jesus. As you talk about 'yourself', make sure that the emphasis is on the part of 'your' life that God made, saved or brought back to life. Explain to the children that the similarity between the characters is that God's power gave them life. The children could

pretend to be other characters that God gave life to, and others could guess who they are.

2 **Prepare**
If you have time, involve the children in making the model for the story. A large group can make more than one model. If you are short of time during the session, make the model(s) in advance. Cut away one long side from the shoebox to make Elisha's room. Stick the table and chair to the walls of the room. Stick the picture of the bed on the matchbox. Mount the characters onto card to make them stronger. Cut the slot in the donkey's back. Use reusable sticky tack to make the figures stand up. (The photo on page 76 shows the finished set of props.).

3 **Story**
Read and enact the story as suggested below. Encourage the children to be involved in moving the characters around and suggesting the dialogue.

Read 2 Kings 4:8: Introduce Elisha, the rich woman and her husband. Pretend that they are talking together.

- **Verses 9,10:** Introduce Elisha's new room.
- **Verses 11–13:** Introduce Gehazi.
- **Verses 14–17:** Bring the woman to Elisha's room and pretend

she is talking to Gehazi and then Elisha. Then move Elisha and Gehazi to another area.
- **Verses 18–21:** Introduce the boy and pretend he is working in the fields with his dad. He falls over and his dad calls for a servant to take him home. Mum then places him on Elisha's bed.
- **Verses 22–24:** Place the woman on the donkey and move them towards Elisha and Gehazi.
- **Verses 25,26:** Elisha talks with Gehazi and Gehazi then runs to the donkey.
- **Verses 27–31:** Move the woman nearer to Elisha. Elisha gives Gehazi the stick (fix it to his hand with sticky tack). Let Gehazi run and lay the stick on the boy's head. The woman and Elisha walk towards the room.
- **Verses 32–34:** Move Elisha as he goes into the room and prays. Then lay him on top of the boy.
- **Verse 35:** Make Elisha walk up and down the room and then lean over the boy's body. Make the boy sit up and sneeze seven times.
- **Verses 36,37:** Make Elisha call out to Gehazi and then move the woman into the room. Make her jump up and down for joy.

Bible story with model

Cut out these items for your model. Glue the characters and donkey on to card.

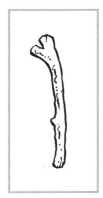

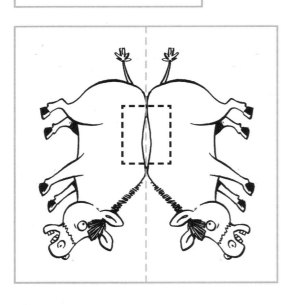

Above: the completed model to use with the Bible story.

CORE PROGRAMME CONTINUED

4 **Reflect**

Encourage the children to say how important the young boy is in this story. Give them time to respond. Ask them what this tells us about God's power and children. Explain that God used his life-giving power in an amazing way because Elisha and the woman trusted God. Ask the children if they have ever trusted God for anything. Allow them time to respond.

Psalm praise

 minutes

Why: to praise our life-giving God

1 Read Psalm 104:24–30 to the children. Challenge them to put together their own psalm to praise God for his life-giving power. They could work together or in pairs.

2 Each contribution could start with the words: 'Thank you, God, for giving life to…' and finish with, 'We praise you, our powerful God!'

3 Allow enough time for everyone to do this. Create the complete 'psalm' by inviting each group in turn to say the lines they have composed.

Trust game

 minutes

Why: to think about what it means to trust

With: three pots – one containing mud, one containing chocolate buttons, one containing baked beans; blindfold; spoons

1 Show everyone the three pots containing mud, chocolate buttons and baked beans. Explain that you are going to blindfold someone and feed them something. (Be aware of allergies.) Ask if there is anyone who trusts you enough to do this. Blindfold one volunteer and then feed them the chocolate.

2 Thank the volunteer for trusting you. Explain that it is sometimes hard to trust people, but in today's story we will find out that we can always trust God and that he will not trick us.

Sing with actions

 minutes

Why: to praise God for his power
With: *Reach Up!* CD, or music from page 76

1 Sing together 'King of all' from the *Reach Up!* CD, and praise God for his power. Explain that this song talks about God's power doing amazing things, just as in today's story. Read out the words to help the children focus on them.

2 Play the song again and ask the children to work out some actions to the verse. Children with physical disabilities could perhaps draw

pictures or do hand actions. Allow time to rehearse the actions.

3 Sing the song again, showing the actions and pictures. The children could perhaps think of an appropriate moment to perform it to other groups or before their parents, so others can praise God too.

King of all

You are the King of all, Lord of all,
Boss of all, chief of all.
The one with power,
You are Jesus, King of kings. (x2).

Power over earth and sea,
Power over all I see,
Power over even death,
Power to let me take a breath.
Power to see what's really me,
Power to solve my deepest need,
Power to give me life for
    evermore!

You are the King of all, Lord of all,
Boss of all, chief of all.
The one with power,
You are Jesus, King of kings. (x2)

(Repeat verse and chorus)

Andy Gawn
© Cluckin' Chicken Music

King of all

Andy Gawn

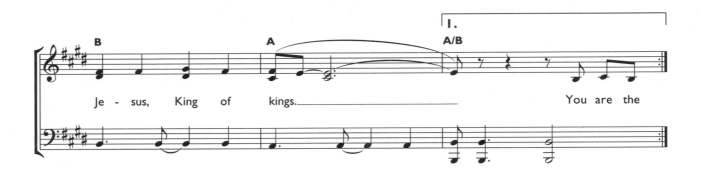

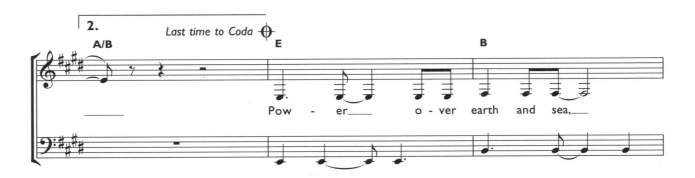

© Cluckin' Chicken Music 2005

EXTENSION IDEAS

Activities for younger children

Poster prayers

(10) *minutes*

Why: to trust God because he is powerful
With: a large sheet of paper

1 In advance, write out the Learn and remember verse from page 94 (Job 42:2) on a large sheet of paper.

2 Read the verse together. Ask: 'Who in today's Bible story trusted in God's power? Who was helped by God's power?'

3 Ask the children to think of something that they need God's power to help with. Encourage them to write or draw their idea on a sticky note. Explain that they are going to trust in God for these things, and invite them to place their sticky note on the poster.

4 Remind the children that God is interested in helping everyone of any age; all we need to do is trust in him. Pray that God will help us trust in him and that we will see his power working in our lives.

Bible story picture

Why: to realise that God wants us to share what we have
With: a copy of page 79 (also available from *LightLive*) printed on A4 paper for each child, art and craft materials

1 Look around you: can you see the walls that make a room? Ask, 'Who can find a chair? And a light? Can anyone find somewhere where they could sleep?'

2 Now look at the Bible story picture. Can the children find a room? Somewhere to sit and sleep?

3 Look at the three people just outside this room. There are a husband and wife standing together. The other man is called Elisha. Do the children know what is happening in this scene?

4 Either read today's Bible story to explain or say that these kind people have built this special room, just for Elisha. It is their way of helping him do his work for God. He will have somewhere warm and comfortable to stay, when he is going from place to place.

For older children

Prayer

(10) *minutes*

Why: to learn to trust God
With: copies of the prayer words on page 78

1 Give each child a copy of page 78. The prayer outline is as follows:

God, you are powerful, you...
(add examples of God's power)

Sometimes I feel...
(negative emotions)

Especially when...
(examples of bad things)

Help me to trust you to...

You are a powerful life-giver!

Amen.

2 Ask the children to 'fill in the gaps' with written or drawn prayers, working individually so that they can think about their own worries or difficult situations. Allow time for the children to pray silently about what they have written or drawn.

THE LEARN AND REMEMBER VERSE

'I know, Lord, /
that you are /
all-powerful; /
that you can do /
everything you want.' /
Job 42:2

Display the words of the verse for the children to see and invite them to sit in a circle and form pairs or threes where they are sitting. In turn, point at each small group around the circle and encourage them to say the next phrase from the verse, as indicated above. Keep going around the circle, so that the verse is said several times.

Find a poster for this Learn and remember verse on page 95.

Alternatively, use the song 'Everything you want' on the *Bitesize Bible Songs 2* CD, available from Scripture Union.

Prayer speech bubble

God,

You are powerful, you

....

Sometimes I feel

....

Especially when

....

Help me to trust you to

....

You are a powerful life-giver!

Amen.

A home for Elisha

SERIES 3 ELISHA THE PROPHET

SESSION 3
Powerful healer

Bible:
2 Kings 5

Aim: To trust God who is the powerful healer

CORE PROGRAMME

For 3-14s

Bible story with actions

 -  *minutes*

Why: to trust God who is the powerful healer
With: SU *Bible Timeline*, labels for the Bible story, props such as a chair for the king's throne, blue cloth for river (all optional)

1 **Prepare**
Make and display labels saying 'Naaman's home', 'Israel's palace', 'Elisha's house' and 'River bank' around the room, making sure there is sufficient space for the children at each place. If you are in a small room, hold up the labels instead of moving to them.

2 *Bible Timeline*
Invite the children to look at the *Bible Timeline* and find a name that they recognise. Encourage them to say something about that person. Ask: 'Did anyone find Elisha?' Challenge someone to find his name now. Ask the children to tell you what they can remember about

Elisha from the previous session. Say that today they will be hearing about Elisha later in the story.

3 **Rhyme**
Tell the children that they can act out as much of the story and be as many of the characters as they wish. Some suggested actions are included in brackets.

Teach the following rhyme, saying that it comes in the story several times:

**Now don't get fussed,
But let's just trust
In God the powerful healer.**

4 **Listen and join in**
Story: *(Gather at 'Naaman's home'.)* **Naaman was a great soldier in the Syrian army.** *(Stand tall and look strong.)* **But he had a secret that only a few people knew. He had a skin disease, which was not likely to get better. In fact, it would get worse and soon he would not be able to live at home any more.** *(Inspect the skin on your arm with a worried look on your face.)*

Naaman had a servant girl who had been captured from Israel. *(Act sweeping, dusting.)* **When she heard about Naaman's illness, she said that Israel's God could heal him - through his prophet, Elisha. 'Now don't get fussed...'**

When the king of Syria heard what the servant girl said, he sent his soldier Naaman off to the king of Israel. *(All travel to 'Israel's palace'.)* **The king of Israel was worried when he read the king of Syria's letter.** *('Tear' hair and look horrified.)* **He knew he could not cure Naaman. He had forgotten all about God. 'Now don't get fussed...'**

Elisha, the prophet, heard what was happening and he sent a message for Naaman to come to his house. *(All travel to 'Elisha's house'.)* **Elisha knew God could heal. 'Now don't get fussed...'**

Elisha's servant came out to say that Naaman was to wash himself seven times in the River Jordan, and then he would be cured. Naaman was furious! *(Stamp feet and cross arms, making an angry face.)* **He thought Elisha should have done something special for him.**

Naaman's servants were upset. They wanted to see their master better, however it happened. They pleaded with him to do as Elisha said. *(Make pleading movements.)* **'Now don't get fussed...'**

CORE PROGRAMME CONTINUED

So Naaman went to the river *(move to the 'river bank')* **and washed himself seven times.** *(Dip down seven times, making washing actions.)* **When he came out of the water the last time, he was completely healed.** *(Stretch arms and smile broadly.)* **Now he knew it was true that God can heal. 'Now don't get fussed…'**

5 Think and pray
Suggest that the children sit quietly at one of the places in the story and talk to God on their own or simply think about what happened. Finish by saying the rhyme one more time together: 'Now don't get fussed…'

Creative prayer
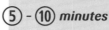 *minutes*

Why: to pray for people who are ill or in need
With: a pot of bubble mix

1 Encourage the children to think of people who are ill or in need – like the soldier in the story – for whom they want to pray. Ask them to write the names of these people on separate sheets of paper. Invite them to fold the sheets of paper and place them in the middle of the floor, saying the person's name if they want to.

2 Talk to the children about how water is cleansing. Introduce the bubbles as a symbol of God's healing.

3 Stand in a circle round the sheets of paper, taking it in turns to blow bubbles and pray for the names on the paper. Finish by saying, 'Our powerful healer God, please care for these people and heal those who are ill.'

Prayer challenge
(5) – (10) *minutes*

Why: to trust God, the powerful healer
With: copies of the diary page from page 82 (optional)

1 Ask the children to draw and label seven boxes for days of the week on a sheet of paper, or give them a copy of the diary page. Invite each child to think of one person who is sick and who they could pray for. Encourage them to write the person's name or draw them on their page.

2 Ask: 'How many times did Naaman have to wash in the river?' (Seven) Emphasise that Naaman had to keep trusting in order to be healed. Find out: 'How many days are there in a week?' Say that God wants us to keep trusting him, too. Challenge them to pray for one person every day for the next week and tick when they have prayed. Remember to have a report-back time, next time you meet!

Cheerleading
 *minutes*

Why: to remember that we can trust God
With: pom-poms, wavers, twirling batons and so on (optional)

1 Divide the children into pairs or small groups. Encourage them to make up a routine (similar to those of cheerleaders at sports events) about the idea of trusting God. Children who have difficulty moving about could clap or wave pom-poms.

2 The children could use: 'T R U S T – we trust God!' or the rhyme from 'Bible story with actions', or make up their own words.

3 Invite the groups to watch all the routines through first, and then to join in with each other's.

4 Remind the children that the words of their routines will help them remember throughout the coming week that they can trust God.

Diary page

I will pray for

Tick the days below you remembered to pray.

Sunday   Monday   Tuesday   Wednesday

Thursday   Friday   Saturday

EXTENSION IDEAS

Activities for younger children

Naaman model

 minutes

Why: to be amazed at what God can do
With: copies of page 84, pens and pencils, sticky tape or glue, scissors, cardboard tubes about 20 cm long

1 Make a copy of page 84 for each child in your group. Each child will also need a cardboard tube.

2 Let the children colour in the picture of Naaman; help them to cut out the shape. There are two Naamans on the page: one shows Naaman before God healed him; turn the picture the other way up and see Naaman after God made him better. Can the children see which is which? Talk about how amazing God is: we can draw Naaman sick and well, but God actually made him better!

3 Show the children how to wrap the picture around a cardboard tube and stick it in place to make a puppet of Naaman. Stand the puppet one way to show Naaman ill; turn it up the other way to show him well again.

4 Use the puppets to tell the story again, and to think about what God can do. What do the children think about God? How do they react to God making Naaman well again?

Bible story picture

Why: to be impressed at what God can do
With: a copy of page 86 (also available from *LightLive*) printed on A4 paper for each child, art and craft materials, water colours, paintbrushes, clean water, cover-up and clean-up facilities

1 Give out copies of the Bible-story picture. Tell the children that Naaman, the man in the river, was not very well. His skin was sore and there was nothing the doctors could

do to make him well again. Let the children paint Naaman, using thin water colour paints, to show how poorly he was.

2 Say that God made Naaman better. Elisha told Naaman to wash seven times in the river. Count slowly from one to seven.

3 On 'seven', brush over the painted Naamans with plenty of clean water, so the paint is diluted and fades away. See how God made Naaman well again, when Naaman did as Elisha said.

For older children

Creative

 minutes

Why: to perform the key point of the passage
With: copies of the drama script on page 85

1 Photocopy the drama script for everyone.

2 Read it through a number of times with different people playing the parts, then decide who the actors are going to be.

3 If you have time, allow time for a short rehearsal and then perform the drama. If the actors are willing, offer to perform the sketch in front of a church audience on some other occasion.

4 Close in prayer, asking for God's healing power for anyone the young people know who is sick.

THE LEARN AND REMEMBER VERSE

'I know, Lord, /
that you are /
all-powerful; /
that you can do /
everything you want.' /
Job 42:2

Find the words of the Learn and remember verse from the poster on page 95. Repeat the verse with different children saying a phrase each. Then, at the end, encourage everyone to shout, 'Yes!' and punch the air with their fist, to show how amazing our powerful God is.

Alternatively, use the song 'Everything you want' on the *Bitesize Bible Songs 2* CD, available from Scripture Union.

Naaman

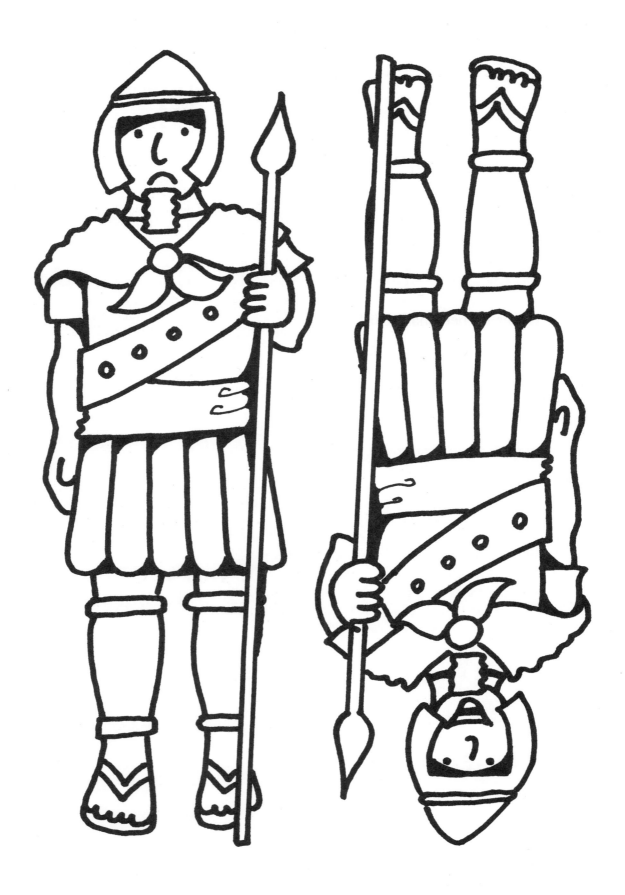

Creative drama script

Set: a shop
Props: a price list and a table
Cast: assistant and customer

Assistant: Good morning. How can I help you?

Customer: I'd like to know how much a miracle would cost.

Assistant: An act of God?

Customer: Indeed.

Assistant: Is this a personal miracle, or is it for a friend?

Customer: Oh, er, it's personal. Selfish of me, I guess.

Assistant: Not to worry. We have many customers after personal miracles.

Customer: Excellent. How does it work then?

Assistant: What currency are you intending to settle in?

Customer: Hmm. Hadn't given it much thought. Do you accept UK pounds?

Assistant: (Checking list.) No, I'm sorry.

Customer: Euros?

Assistant: (Laughing without checking.) No, of course not.

Customer: Dollars?

Assistant: (Checking list.) Well, we used to. They do say 'In God we trust' but our research has cast some doubt on that.

Customer: So?

Assistant: So, no.

Customer: What currencies do you accept?

Assistant: Well, not really monetary ones.

Customer: I see. So I could pay back with service. Payment by works?

Assistant: No, we don't accept that any more.

Customer: Commitment?

Assistant: No.

Customer: Worship?

Assistant: No.

Customer: Faith?

Assistant: Faith?

Customer: Faith?

Assistant: You have some faith?

Customer: A little.

Assistant: Oh, that will do nicely.

Elisha and Naaman

SESSION 4
Powerful warrior

Bible:
2 Kings 6:8–23

Aim: To be confident because our God is a powerful warrior

CORE PROGRAMME

For 3-14s

Musical Bible story

20 *minutes*

Why: to be confident because our God is a powerful warrior
With: a selection of musical instruments, SU *Bible Timeline* (optional)

1 In advance
If possible, contact some of the children and ask them to bring in any musical instruments they have or can play. If they don't have any, they could make some percussion instruments, such as shakers out of yogurt pots and lentils. Make sure you bring in some instruments yourself, or things that can be used as such, for example, wooden and metal spoons, pans, boxes, party blowers, football rattles, whistles and plastic beakers (for horses' hooves!).

2 Listen
Tell the children to listen carefully as you read from the Bible, as they are going to be retelling the story using

musical instruments. Read 2 Kings 6:8–23 from a child-friendly Bible. If possible, get another leader to read it with you, with one of you being the narrator and the other doing different voices for the other characters.

3 Create
Put the children into groups, and invite each group to take it in turns to pick an instrument until everyone has one.

Challenge the groups to use their instruments to retell the story. Move around the groups, helping them develop their ideas. They will undoubtedly be creating great masterpieces, but here are some suggestions for you of what sorts of noises or music can be created.

- **2 Kings 6:8:** Noise of war, then quiet for the start of the council meeting.
- **2 Kings 6:9:** Use quiet instruments to be 'voices'.
- **2 Kings 6:11:** Use a loud noise to indicate the king's anger.
- **2 Kings 6:14:** Noise of horses and chariots.
- **2 Kings 6:15:** Drum roll noises to show Elisha's servant's fear.
- **2 Kings 6:16:** Calm or strong noises to show Elisha's confidence in God.
- **2 Kings 6:18,19:** Banging noises as the people are blinded.

- **2 Kings 6:20:** Crescendo as the army's eyes are opened in Samaria.
- **2 Kings 6:23:** Lots of celebratory noises for the feast.

4 Perform and reflect
Invite the groups to listen to each other perform the story.

Explain that using a variety of instruments to tell the story shows us that the story is very dramatic. Ask them why they think the story is dramatic. What do they think this story tells us about God?

5 Bible Timeline
See if the children can guess where on the *Bible Timeline* today's story comes.

Chat and mime

5 - **10** *minutes*

Why: to think about what a powerful warrior is like
With: a copy of the person outline from page 89

1 Show the person outline to the group (or draw a larger version yourself).

2 Encourage the children to imagine that the person in the outline is a soldier. He is there to protect, rather than to fight. Ask for words describing what he might be like, and write these on his body, for example, 'strong' and 'able to carry' (on his arms), 'fast' and 'powerful' (on his legs), 'loving' (on his heart), 'speaking' or 'putting right' (on his mouth).

3 Call out different parts of the soldier's body and challenge the children to mime appropriate actions. Keep the outline for the 'Warrior prayer' activity.

Warrior prayer

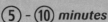 minutes

Why: to thank God because he is a powerful warrior
With: the person outline from page 89

1 Encourage the children to look at the picture of the protecting warrior from 'Chat and mime' again. Suggest that, as you read the words together, they remember that God is a powerful warrior. Ask: 'Which of these things did God show in today's story?' and 'Can you think of times when he has shown any of the other characteristics?' Invite the children to share their own stories of when God has helped them.

2 Teach the refrain: 'Thank you, God, that we can have confidence in you.' Suggest that each child thanks God for one of the warrior attributes on the picture (such as: speaking, strong, loving, able to carry, powerful, fast), saying the refrain together each time.

Collage

 – *minutes*

Why: to think about power
With: magazines, marker pens (all optional)

1 Challenge the children to call out anything they can think of to do with the word 'power'.

2 Invite them to make a 'power collage' as a group, using the words they have thought of. They could add pictures from magazines, or draw their own pictures of powerful people and things.

3 If God is not already on the collage, ask the children if they think he should be, and why. Encourage them to write 'God' in big letters on their poster. Say that in today's story they will find out how some people discover how powerful God really is.

Person outline

EXTENSION IDEAS

Activities for younger children

Make a visor

 minutes

Why: to remember the Bible story and that God can do anything
With: visors from page 92 photocopied onto thin card, elastic thread, glitter pens, hole punch (optional)

1 Cut out the visors. Remind the children of God's soldiers. Elisha knew they were protecting him and he prayed so that his servant could see them too. Let the children colour God's soldiers as brightly as they can.

2 Put away the bright colours and just leave green and brown colours. Turn the visors over. Remind the children that the enemy soldiers could not see God's soldiers. They could just see countryside. Ask the children to colour this side of the visor to show grass and trees.

3 Punch a hole in each end of the visors and tie elastic thread to fit each child's head. The children should wear the visors with the soldiers inside. This way, they can see God's soldiers, while everyone else can just see countryside!

THE LEARN AND REMEMBER VERSE

'I know, LORD, /
that you are /
all-powerful; /
that you can do /
everything you want.' /
Job 42:2

Bible story picture

Why: to discover that God can do anything
With: a copy of page 94 (also available from *LightLive*) printed on A4 paper for each child, art and craft materials including collage scraps and glue

1 Give out copies of the Bible story picture and basic crayons or colouring pencils.

2 Say that Elisha was not afraid of soldiers coming to hurt him because he knew that God's army was keeping him safe.

3 Provide as many exciting and exotic collage materials as you can, so the children can make God's army dazzle!

For older children

Imaginative prayer

 minutes

Why: to ask for God's powerful protection for the local community
With: chairs, copies of the sword outline from page 93

1 Invite the children to sit in rows with their sword outlines as if they are in a minibus. (Use chairs if you have some.)

2 Challenge the children to imagine they are on a journey around your local area. Get them to close their eyes and talk them through an imaginary trip, describing the route out loud.

3 Pause as you come to various places such as the school, a park, shops and the post office. Encourage the children to hold up their swords and imagine the army that Elisha and his servant saw in the story. Invite them silently to ask God to protect, with his power, all the people who go to this place, just as he powerfully protected Elisha and his servant.

Divide the children into two groups. Give each group part of the verse to invent some actions for. Read the verse out so that each group can show their actions. Invite each group to teach the others their actions, and then challenge everyone to say the whole verse with all the actions.

Find a poster for this Learn and remember verse on page 95.

Alternatively, use the song 'Everything you want' on the *Bitesize Bible Songs 2* CD, available from Scripture Union.

Make a visor template

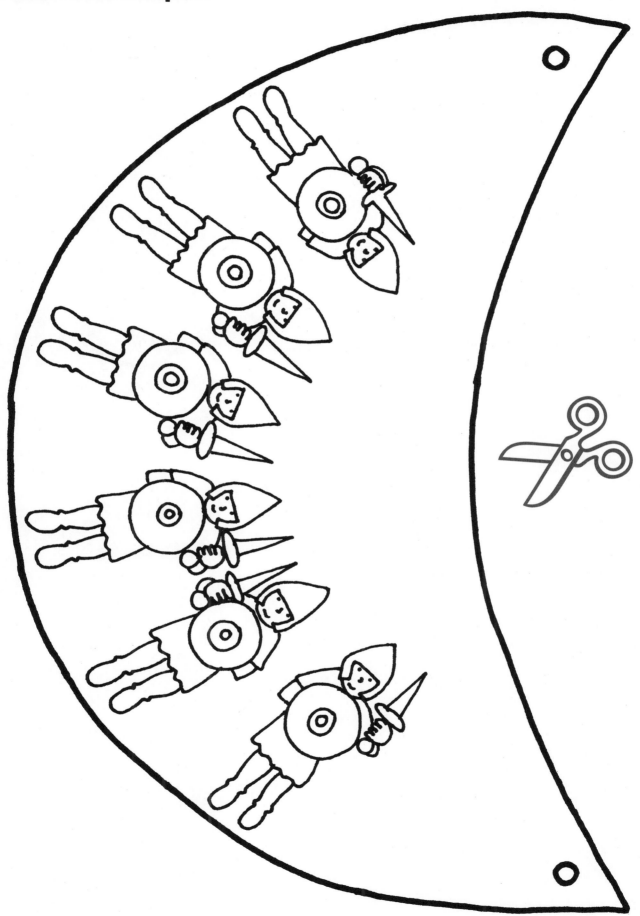

Sword for imaginative prayer

Elisha prays

'I know, Lord, that you are all-powerful; that you can do everything you want.'

Job 42:2

What's next?

Look out for *Mosaic* resource *God is good* which contains 12 more sessions for your small group with mixed ages.

Discover how God protects David in his early life in the series **In God's hands**.

See how Jesus' parables confront us with challenges about how we should live in the series **Jesus challenges us**.

Find out more about the God who communicates with us, using stories from the early chapters of Acts in **Adventures with God**.

Plus a bonus all-age service based on **Psalm 23**.

You can obtain this book and many other Scripture Union resources online by visiting **www.scriptureunion.org.uk/shop**

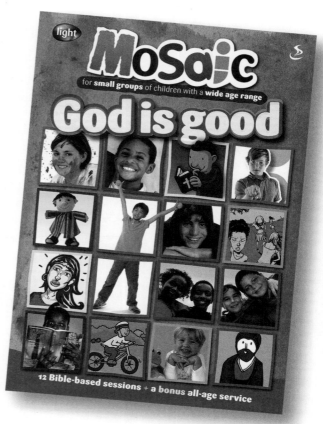

 online

For weekly online resources for your group, take a look at *Mosaic* online at **www.scriptureunion.org.uk/lightlive**. Creating a *Mosaic* group will enable you to browse through all the downloadable resources.